UTOPIA

UTOPIA

▼

Heaven or Hell?

Orville H. Schmidt

Writers Club Press
San Jose New York Lincoln Shanghai

Utopia
Heaven or Hell?

Writers Club Press
an imprint of iUniverse.com, Inc.

For information address:
iUniverse.com, Inc.
5220 S 16th, Ste. 200
Lincoln, NE 68512
www.iuniverse.com

ISBN: 0-595-18391-3

Printed in the United States of America

CONTENTS

Chapter One The Dream Previewed 1
   Definitions..*1*
   Why Study Utopia? *3*
   Nature of Utopian Thought *3*
   Origins of Utopian Thought *6*

Chapter Two The Dream Surveyed: Utopias In History 9
   Biblical World *9*
   Classical World..................................*10*
   Medieval World *13*
   Renaissance *14*

Chapter Three The Dream Surveyed: Utopia and Technology 23
   Technological Utopias..........................*23*
   The Rejection of Technology *29*

Chapter Four The Dream Surveyed: Utopia and Economics 39
   Utopian Capitalism *39*
   Utopian Socialism *43*
   Mixed Varieties *51*

Chapter Five   The Dream Surveyed: Utopia and Territory 53
    Minitopias...*53*
    Miditopias...*55*
    Maxitopias..*56*
    Globalopia..*64*

Chapter Six   The Dream Perverted 69
    Evolutionary Dystopias..*69*
    Behavioralistic Dystopias...*73*
    Totalitarian Dystopias *80*

Chapter Seven The Dream Revisited 91
    Is the Dream Possible?..*91*
    Is the Dream Desirable? *93*
    Redefinition of Utopia *94*

About the Author 97

Bibliography 99

CHAPTER ONE

▼

THE DREAM PREVIEWED

DEFINITIONS. Ever since Thomas More, writers have had difficulties in defining utopia. He combined the Greek words *ou* (no) and *topos* (place) but used the Latin spelling, *utopia.* It may be said that since *outopia* is a "no place" while *eutopia* is a "good place," *utopia* then is a "good no place!" Is it merely a dream? Is the dream possible? If utopia is a place without problems, is not this itself a problem? Then too, there is the matter of subjectivity. One man's utopia may be another man's dystopia, one man's heaven another man's hell.

In the most simplistic terms, a utopia may be defined as a place where people are happy and have free will. A dystopia may be defined as a place where people are not happy or if they are happy they do not have free will as the people in the **Brave New World** of Aldous Huxley.

Three other writers who seemed to think of utopia as a "no place" were Karl Marx, Friedrich Engels, and Karl Mannheim. While Marx and Engels themselves sought an ideal world order, they called the non-revolutionary socialists of the 18th and 19th centuries utopian since they themselves did not believe the ideal society could be achieved without revolution. Likewise, Karl Mannheim believed that utopias were, in effect, unimplemented value systems whereas ideologies were value systems that had been implemented.

Lewis Mumford, on the other hand, distinguishes in **The Story of Utopias** (1922), between utopias of escape (impossible dreams) and utopias of reconstruction (possible dreams). The former prevent us from achieving the ideal society whereas the latter help us to attain it. As Oscar Wilde put it in **The Soul of Man Under Socialism**, "A map of the world that does not include Utopia is not worth even glancing at, for it leaves out the one country at which Humanity is always landing. And when Humanity lands there, it looks out, and seeing a better country, sets sail. Progress is the realization of Utopias." In **The Devil's Dictionary** (1911), Ambrose Bierce gives a definition of a fool which in many ways applies to the utopist. "A person who pervades the domain of intellectual speculation and diffuses himself through the channels of moral activity. He is omnific, omniform, omniperscipient, omniscient, omnipotent. He it was who invented letters, printing, the railroad, the steamboat, the telegraph, the platitude and the circle of sciences. He created patriotism and taught nations war, founded theology, philosophy, law, medicine, and Chicago. He established monarchical and republican government. He is from everlasting to everlasting—such as creation's dawn beheld he fooleth now. In the morning of time he sang upon primitive hills, and in the noonday of existence headed the procession of being. His grandmotherly hand has warmly tucked in the set sun of civilization and in the twilight he prepares man's evening meal of milk and morality and turns down the covers of the universal grave. And after the rest of us shall have returned for the night of eternal oblivion he will sit up to write a history of civilization."

WHY STUDY UTOPIA? It is for this purpose of reconstruction that the study of utopian literature is so important. Such views provide us with a model for creating a better world and encourage us to get on with the task. Better to have tried and failed than never to have failed at all! But even if the various fictional utopias are impossible dreams, a careful examination of them is by no means a frivolous enterprise. First, much of the greatest literature in the world is utopian in character. We cannot be fully aware of our cultural heritage if we ignore all of the great utopian works. Second, the study of utopias often helps us to get a better perspective. One of the capitalist persuasion, for example, by studying socialist utopias may come to better understand the flaws in capitalism. The reverse is also true since not all utopias are socialistic. A student of agrarian utopias may more fully understand the vast problems of industrialism. Finally, utopian thought has made positive contributions to the development of institutions. The American founding fathers, for example, were inspired to a great degree by Harrington's **The Commonwealth of Oceana** (1656). The British Royal Society was inspired by Bacon's "House of Salomon" in the New Atlantis .

NATURE OF UTOPIAN THOUGHT. In **From Utopia to Nightmare** (1962), Chad Walsh compares the Bourbon to the

Jacobin traditions. The latter "is the great theorizer, the planner, the apostle of the *tabula rasa*. He wonders why one should tinker in trivial ways with society. Why not sit down, take a long look at the social scene, meditate on first principles, and draw up blueprints? The spirit that moves the Jacobin is Why? He demands that each feature of the social organism present its rational credentials. Indeed, he is reluctant to use the word organism. To him society is rather an organization, based ultimately on the social contract. He is at ease with written constitutions and formal rules and regulation, for these can be rationally debated, amended, and even supplanted. He is bewildered and irritated by the vague but exceedingly persistent network of subtle attitudes, habits, customs, ways of doing things." The Bourbon, on the other hand, is very anti-utopian. He has a deep-felt sense of the complexity and rootedness of any society, and is extremely reluctant to change anything in it, for fear that the delicate plant will be mortally injured. He is likely to be strong on intuition, weak on critical analysis. He prefers the evils that he himself recognizes to the unknown evils that may ensue if the organism is tampered with. He is willing to tolerate a multitude of apparent absurdities, even though he cannot say what purpose they serve. He senses, in a way he can seldom articulate, that they are part of the total organism as it has evolved, and though he cannot prove that they have any use, this does not prove the contrary…(he knows) that society is not a mechanism but an organism, with an internal logic; that its various features fit together in a weird and wonderful way, that the surgeon who wishes to remove one part or graft another into the social body had better be sure he knows what he is doing."

Most utopian writers are optimistic. Walsh further suggests nine characteristics of the utopist. He believes man (1) is good, (2) is malleable, (3) is rational, (4) can live in harmony with society, (5) can anticipate to some degree the future, (6) can achieve earthly welfare, (7) does not find happiness boring, (8) can find just rulers, and (9) can harmonize freedom with authority. The utopist tends to reject both organized religion and theistic religion, stresses evolution, emphasizes economics, and has faith in the trinity of science, technology, and machinery. He looks to the future rather than to the past and is, by and large, disinterested in history.

In addition to its optimistic strain, utopian thought is holistic. Whereas most writers confine themselves to certain phases of human activity, the utopist is concerned with the whole range of human activity. He asks questions concerning such fields as (1) Political Science: what is the truly ideal form of government? Is there a distinction between human and divine law and, if so, what is the relationship between them? What are the relative merits of elitism and democracy? Is freedom incompatible with planning? Is change incompatible with stability? (2) Economics: Should property be publicly or privately owned? Should all work be paid equally? Should machinery eliminate human labor wherever possible? Should we increase our consumption of material goods? (3) Psychology: Is man emotional or rational, a mechanism or an organism, a creature of free will or one whose existence is determined by external forces? (4) Sociology: what is the impact of technology on society? What should be the relationship between the individual and society? How should the generational gap be dealt with? What is the role of women in society? (5) Family Life: Should marriages be lifetime commitments on renewable contracts? Are group marriages preferable to the nuclear family? Is pre-marital and extramarital sex permissible? Should human mating be determined by eugenics rather than by love? Should children be reared in the home or away from home? (6) Education: Should the schools be traditional or progressive, elitist or democratic? (7) Culture: Should art, literature, and music have only functional or also esthetic purposes? (8) Theology: Is religion or secularism the surest road to utopia? Is there a God and, if so, is this God immanent or transcendent?

ORIGINS OF UTOPIAN THOUGHT. One source of utopian thought has already been noted, that is man's need to dream. Only if he has his eyes on the stars does life in the mud become tolerable. Thoreau points out in **Walden** that we must first dream our castles in the air before we begin to put foundations under them. A second inspiration of utopian thought is historical experience. After every political or social upheaval there emerges a good deal of utopian literature. The Pelopponesian War was followed by Plato, the Babylonian Captivity by Jeremiah, the collapse of the Roman Empire by Augustine. The Reformation and Renaissance produced writers such as Andreae and More, the Industrial Revolution preceded the Utopian Socialists and Marxists. In the 20th century, catastrophes such as two world wars, a worldwide depression, and the rise of totalitarian regimes led to dystopian literature by Zamiatin, Huxley, and Orwell.

Perhaps a third major source of utopian thought is theological in nature. Whether one takes the biblical account of creation literally or not, it certainly suggests that when man was first created he did live in a utopian situation. Many Christian theologians believe that man's fall into sin led not only to his expulsion from utopia but to his sinful desire to recreate utopia without the help of God. This story of the fall has been secularized by the liberal and socialist intellectuals of the

18th and 19th centuries who also envisioned man as once having lived in an ideal state but who somehow corrupted himself. Such writers, of course, believe that the utopian ideal is attainable. If man will destroy the non-utopian institutions he has created (the state and private property), he can recover his utopian nature. An interesting, if possibly heretical interpretation of the story of the story of creation, is presented in the movie Westworld. It is about a resort in which robots provide for every need and pleasure of man but who because of malfunctions begin to operate as autonomous creatures, thus creating a dystopian world. As will be seen later, Ayn Rand sees man in the Garden of Eden as a robot. Instead, however, of seeing his rebellion against God as a malfunction of his nature, she sees it as an affirmation of a higher nature. Man acquires human dignity only by his rebellion against God.

CHAPTER TWO

▼

THE DREAM SURVEYED: UTOPIAS IN HISTORY

BIBLICAL WORLD. Various prophets in the Old Testament hold out utopian visions. In **Amos 9:14(Good News Bible)**. God says, "I will bring my people back to their land. They will rebuild their ruined cities and live there, they will plant vineyards and drink the wine; they will plant gardens and eat what they grow." In **Jeremiah 23:3-4,** He further says, "I will gather the rest of my people from the countries where I have scattered them, and I will bring them back to their homeland. They will have many children and will increase in number. I will appoint rulers to take care of them. My people will no longer be afraid or terrified, and I will not punish them again. I, the Lord, have spoken." A most beautiful vision of utopia is in **Isaiah 35:5-7,** "The blind will be able to see, and the deaf hear. The lame will leap and dance and those who cannot speak will shout for joy. Streams of water will flow through the desert; the burning sand will become a lake." Also in **Isaiah 2:4**, "They will hammer their swords into plows and their spears into pruning knives. Nations will never again go to war, never prepare for battle again." Some of these are obviously heavenly utopias but have inspired secular utopian thought.

The New Testament Christians practiced a form of communism. Luke says in **Acts 4:34-35**, "There was no one in the group who was in need. Those who owned fields or houses would sell them, bring the money received from the sale and turn it over to the apostles; and the money was distributed to each according to his need." John speaks in **Revelation 20**, of a millennium in which Christ shall rule a thousand years on earth. The Jehovah Witnesses interpret this literally and assume there will be a utopia on earth.

CLASSICAL WORLD. In **The Parallel Lives**, Plutarch describes the Spartan constitution drawn up by Lycurgus, sometimes considered to be the model for Plato's utopia. This provided for a rather austere military communism. The government of two kings and twenty-eight senators anticipated the American separation of powers principle. Land reform was effected. There were 9,000 equal plots of land for the members of the upper class; 30,000 equal plots of land for the members of the lower classes. Money was made of iron so as to discourage its use. All unprofitable and superfluous arts were excluded. The people ate in common mess halls, partly to discourage waste, partly to encourage consumption of simple foods. Both men and women were required to undergo rigorous physical training. Extramarital sex was permitted between consenting adults, when it might contribute to the breeding of more excellent children.

Lawyers were not permitted. (It is interesting to note that virtually all utopias are agreed that there would be no lawyers, presumably since the latter must perpetuate conflicts to make work for themselves.) Travel outside of Sparta was greatly discouraged since it was feared some citizens might return corrupted.

Plato's **Republic** (c. 387 BC) is one of the most famous designs for utopia. Plato began by asking "What is the just state?" For Plato, it was the one in which each citizen was permitted to do that for which he was best fitted. This was achieved by a threefold classification: (1) those who desired only the creature comforts of life, (2) those who desired adventure or danger, and (3) those who enjoyed intellectual and speculative enterprises. The first were the workers, the second the policemen and soldiers, and the third were the philosopher-kings. It was an elitist society managed by the latter group who determined into which group people were placed. There was some social mobility in that children from one group might be promoted to another group.

There was communism of property but only for the philosopher-kings. In most societies, there is a variant form of the golden rule at work, "He who has the gold makes the rules." The reverse may also be true. "He who makes the rules gets the gold." Plato denied both. He tried to separate politics from economics fearing that power corrupts and that people in power might abuse that power for personal gain. Similarly, the philosopher-kings were not permitted private family life for they would be distracted by family cares and tempted to create dynasties. Wives and children were held in common. Mating was arranged for eugenic purposes. Children were reared in public nurseries since parents were too emotionally involved to raise them. It also provided an opportunity for indoctrination. Education stressed both intellectual and physical training. Music and athletics, in particular, were emphasized since they both promoted harmony within the individual. Although the philosopher-kings were denied private property and family life for fear they might be corrupted, they were generally considered to be all-wise and all-virtuous. Thus there was felt no need for a written constitution. The concept of the philosopher-kings was Plato's greatest contribution to utopian thought. Many subsequent utopias are based on this elitist principle.

Aristotle, a student of Plato, criticized his teacher both with respect to the communist and elitist principles. He believed that property that belongs to everyone belongs to no one since there is no individual pride of ownership. At the same time, he rejected an elitist system in which a few leaders managed everything for that would incite revolution among the people. He favored a system in which there was some inequity but no gross maldistribution of wealth. Government should not be by philosopher-kings, but based on a balance of power principle with both the rich and the poor having something to say about government. Officials should be limited in their power by written constitutions.

A somewhat less austere utopia than those of Lycurgus and Plato was the **Ecclesiazusae** of Aristophanes (c. 393 BC). Women took over the meeting place and created a totally communistic society. It was one of abundance in which no one lacked the daily needs of life. There was sexual communism in that any consenting adults were free to have sexual relations. Some proponents of communism of property believe this is not possible without sexual communism.

Where there are private families there will be a desire for private property to provide for them. At the same time, most utopias are concerned with order. It is difficult to see how sexual anarchy would not lead to political anarchy.

Among the Stoics there were some broad utopian notions if not too much in the way of specific descriptions. Among these was the notion that the universe was ruled by divine reason (essentially a pantheistic doctrine) and that we are all members of a universal family. Seneca believed that our primary loyalty must be to the universal moral commonwealth rather than to the particular political commonwealth in which we all live. He stressed a natural communism (land, just as air and water, belonged to everybody).

MIDDLE AGES. During the medieval era, men looked forward to a heavenly rather than an earthly utopia. St. Augustine in **The City of God** or **Civitas Dei** (written between 413 and 426) saw utopia more as a state of mind, "The kingdom of God within us." We should then be free of all passion and lust, dedicated to the service of God and our fellowmen. Despairing of self we should cast all care upon God. In such a society, utopia would exist spontaneously. There would be no need to institutionalize it.

A somewhat more earthly utopia was envisaged by Joachim of Flora. He first developed the triadic view of history, later developed in the dialectical process of Hegel and Marx (discussed in Chapter Five). The Age of the Father was represented by the Old Testament. This was the period of patriarchs and kings with the emphasis on authority. The Age of the Son was the period of freedom and peace. The Age of the Spirit (beginning in 1260) was the age of friendship and mysticism. The thesis of authority and the antithesis of wisdom (in Christ) were synthesized into a kind of spontaneously good life much like that envisaged by Augustine.

The musical version of Camelot presents a delightful utopia. The weather was always nice, it rained only at night, winters were extremely short, *etcetera*. The Knights of the Round Table in their pursuit of justice were certainly utopian characters. This vision inspired another Camelot, the Kennedy years with the President and First Lady playing the roles of King Arthur and Queen Guinivere. More recent revelations indicating President Kennedy was Lancelot to someone else's Guinivere remind us that infidelity in the original Camelot made it something less than a utopia!

RENAISSANCE. A more concrete model of utopia was created by Savaranola. A militant Dominican monk, he created a puritanical government in Florence after the downfall of the Medici, a pattern later emulated by Calvin in Geneva. During his reign, people were encouraged to lead an austere life, merchants were inspired to return ill-gotten gains, churches became very popular, philanthropy flourished. It is reminiscent of Puritan New England and also the People's Republic of China during the Cultural Revolution of the 1960s in which the people did seem to be motivated by a puritanical self-discipline. Eventually, Savaranola alienated the Papacy (at one of its most luxury-loving and corrupt periods), reactionary politicians, and the people themselves who tired of such austerity. He was overthrown, hanged, and his body burned.

Probably the most famous design for an ideal community after the time of Plato was Sir Thomas More's **Utopia** (1516). We have already seen how More, by coining a new word from the Greek words for "no" and "place" gave the connotation to utopia of the impossible dream. More was at one time the Lord Chancellor of England under Henry VIII. He refused to subscribe to the Act of Supremacy by which Henry became head of the Church of England following papal denial of his application for divorce from Katherine of Aragon. As a result, Henry ordered Thomas beheaded.

His work describes a mythical society somewhere in the western hemisphere, supposedly discovered by Raphael Hythloday, a Portuguese adventurer. In the first part of the book, Hythloday comments on existing social conditions in England. He is quite critical of a system which placed property rights over all other civil rights. Under the Enclosure Acts, which forced many peasants off the land, people were considered less important than sheep. He also criticized the harsh penal code. People were often forced into a life of crime by the socioeconomic system and then severely punished. Hythloday says, "I am persuaded that unless private property is entirely done away with, there can be no fair distribution of goods, nor can the world be happily governed. As long as private property remains, the largest and far the best part of mankind will be oppressed with an inescapable load of cares and anxieties." When asked why a philosopher like himself did not enter the service of the king as an advisor, he replied that such people were corrupted by the king.

In the second part of the book, Hythloday describes utopia. It is a simple agrarian society located on a crescent-shaped island. All property is commonly owned. People are required to change their homes every ten years to avoid personal attachments to property.

Homes are simple but attractive, always with a garden. The workday is only six hours since people are encouraged to limit their wants. There is a labor rotation system between country and city so that people will not become bored with their work. While food may be obtained from public storehouses and prepared at home most residents prefer to eat in public dining rooms to enjoy the company of others. Since there is no need for money, gold is used for such things as chamber-pots! There are public hospitals with the best of medical care for everyone. Education is encouraged for all. The religion of the Utopians is a form of pantheism but they are tolerant of other religions. Divorce and euthanasia are both permitted, the latter only with the consent of the person involved and a priest. (This is rather interesting since as a devout Catholic, More must have been opposed to both.) While premarital sex is not permitted, persons contemplating marriage are permitted to inspect each other's body before marriage in the presence of a chaperone of the same sex as the person being inspected.

Politically, Utopia was a democracy. Each city was divided into four quarters or wards, each ward into five precincts, each precinct into ten blocks, each block contained thirty families. Each block elected a magistrate whose main task was to see that no one was idle. Each precinct elected a chief magistrate. The two hundred magistrates in each city elected a "prince" for life but who was subject to impeachment if he abused his powers. The capital city was known as Amaurot.

There were a number of dystopian features in utopia. Travel was severely restricted. The Utopians were imperialists for as the population increased, they would establish colonies on the adjacent mainland. While they tried to avoid war, they used such methods as assassination of enemy leaders once involved. Prisoners became slaves (as did criminals). These slaves were assigned unpleasant tasks such as being butchers. Arthur Morgan (an alumnus of St. Cloud State University when it was still a Normal School) in **Nowhere was Somewhere** (1946) says that More's book was not just fiction but based on accounts he had heard about the Inca Empire in South America. He points out many parallels between Utopia and the Inca Empire.

A century and a half later, James Harrington, described his version of utopia in **The Commonwealth of Oceana** (1656). Harrington was a student of governments, particularly of the Republic of Venice. He was a supporter of Cromwell. The hero of this book, Megaletor, was modeled after Cromwell. Harrington's work was not so much a utopia as a model constitution. He advocated supremacy of laws, the secret ballot, indirect elections, and rotation of office. While not a socialist, he did say that extreme inequities in land tenure should be avoided. Like Aristotle, he feared such inequities would lead to revolution. He also advocated a bicameral legislature with one house confined to debating bills and the other house voting on them. He believed there should be an established church but toleration of other churches. Education was compulsory for children from families with more than one child. The American founding fathers were familiar with Harrington's work and many of his ideas found their way into the American constitution.

A much more frivolous utopia than those of More and Harrington was described by Rabelais in the story of Gargantua (1530). Rabelais was a rather unmonkish monk. He rejected medieval scholasticism, a methodological approach to the acquisition of knowledge just as behavioralism is today. (Perhaps the most famous of scholastics was Thomas Aquinas who synthesized the teachings of Aristotle and Augustine and tried to show that revelation could be explained in terms of reason.) Rabelais rejected scholasticism because of its dogmatic approach, its almost blind worship of authority. He anticipated the more empirical approach of modern times. Like other men of the Renaissance, Rabelais was a universal man; that is, one who was interested in the broad range of human knowledge and who was not a narrow specialist. If he made any contribution to theology it was that humor is a means of grace. Unless we can laugh at ourselves we fall into such despair that we will consider ourselves irredeemable by God and thus commit the one unforgivable sin. Like Luther, Rabelais would say that if one must sin let him sin bravely. We cannot act without sinning but not to act is also a sin for then we can never do anything worthwhile.

Gargantua, the hero, was a mixture of Paul Bunyan and Huckleberry Finn. He was the giant son of giant parents, persons of considerable wealth and station in life. He left home and had many adventures. While gone, he heard of difficulties his parents were having at home, a war among the servants. He returned home and with the help of a Friar John restored order. He then built the Abbey of Thelemë as a reward for Friar John. A lovely chateau was constructed. Both men and women were admitted but only the most intelligent and physically attractive. An endowment was established to provide for all their physical needs, including an army of servants. A motto was placed over the entrance, "Do as thou wilt." No politicians, lawyers, preachers, monks, or bankers were permitted. Great stress was placed on education but in keeping with the modern spirit of academic freedom and empiricism rather than with medieval scholasticism. There seemed to be little concern with social issues.

With the Abbey of Thelemë there was a shift of emphasis, as Lewis Mumford said, from the "good" life to the "goods" life. Stress was placed more on materialistic than on moralistic values. Many of the utopias of the modern era reflect this view.

More serious utopias were those of Campanella and Andreae. Campanella's background was somewhat similar to that of Rabelais. He too was a monk but one who also rejected much of medieval scholasticism. As a result, he had difficulties with the Vatican. His problems were compounded by the fact that he promoted the creation of an independent republic in his home province of Calabria in southern Italy to serve as a model for an ideal world order. As a result, he was accused of treason by the Spanish authorities who at that time occupied this area.

He wrote **The City of the Sun** (1623), an account of a communist utopia somewhere near the equator. Written about a century after More's utopia, it may have been based on accounts of the Maya or Inca Empires. It was built on a hill with seven concentric walls. If the outer wall fell to attack, the defenders could fall back to the next, making it progressively more difficult for the invaders. The walls, however, served a second function. They provided a kind of encyclopedia in that they were covered with a compilation of knowledge: mathematics, geology, botany, zoology, descriptions of scientific inventions, and biographies of famous personages.

The political ruler was called Hoh or Metaphysicus and reflected the philosopher-king principle. He was aided by three ministers: (1) Pon or Power, responsible for all military affairs; (2) Sin or Knowledge, for scientific development; and (3) Mor or Love, for regulation of sexual and family matters. Sex was very minutely regulated. Men must be at least 21 and women 19 to engage in sex for procreation. He recognized sexual needs on the part of younger men who were permitted to have sexual relations with sterile or pregnant women! All property was publicly owned. Since there was no rich class to maintain, no one had to work more than four hours a day. Unlike More's utopia, all work was considered honorable. There was no special class of slaves. Prisons and torture were banned but the death penalty was permitted for rather minor offenses. The great emphasis on technology anticipated many of the modern utopias.

Another theocratic utopia was that described by Johann Andreae in **Christianopolis** (1620). He was a Lutheran pastor very much impressed with Calvinist Geneva. He also appears to have been involved with the founding of the Rosicrucian Society, a mystical group which, like the Lutherans, used as its symbol a cross centered in the heart of a rose. The Rosicrucians put a great deal of emphasis on numerology and astrology and believed in the perfectibility of man, something in which Lutherans certainly did not believe. Evidently he became disenchanted with the Rosicrucians since in later years he was a rather conservative Lutheran.

Andreae's utopia was on a small island known as "Caphar Salama." It was a square city, characterized by the Renaissance love of symmetry. Farms and heavy industry were on the edge of the city. In the interior were separate zones for metal, stone, wood, and textile industries. Here we see the modern concept of zoning. The city was governed by a triumvirate consisting of a minister of religion, a superintendent of education, and a judge. (Probably because of the Lutheran emphasis on original sin, it was not presumed there would be no crime as it was in many other utopias.) These three rulers were assisted by twenty-four councilors. The former were the executive branch, the latter the legislature. Bureaucrats were chosen by a merit system. There were public storehouses where all citizens could obtain their needs. Since family life was stressed, meals were prepared and eaten at home in contrast to the public dining halls of More and Campanella. The educational philosophy stressed, in a typically Lutheran fashion, the unity of family, state, and church. To provide intellectual leadership there was a College of Scholars and, as with Campanella, emphasis was placed on scientific and technological training. Marriage was primarily for procreative purposes. Andreae made no provision for premarital sex as did Campanella. Women could not vote although they were equally educated with men.

In summary, one can here see a steady progress toward the technological utopias of the future. More, Harrington, and Rabelais all stressed education but of a humanistic nature. With Campanella and Andreae, more stress was placed on the natural sciences. This evolution towards technological utopias culminated in the science-fiction type of dystopias such as **We** and the **Brave New World.**

CHAPTER THREE

▼

THE DREAM SURVEYED: UTOPIA AND TECHNOLOGY

TECHNOLOGICAL UTOPIAS. As will be seen in the next chapter, there are both socialistic and capitalistic utopias. Both are interested in promoting the "goods" life. In the former, this was achieved by giving everyone an equal piece of the pie. In the latter, it is done by creating a bigger pie. This was the approach of Francis Bacon's **New Atlantis** (1627). The way to create the bigger pie was by technology.

Like Thomas More, Bacon served as the Lord Chancellor of England (under James I). He too got into trouble with the king but due to his own greed. He was convicted of bribery. Following the remission of his sentence, he spent the remainder of his life in scientific activities. Like Rabelais and Campanella, he rejected medieval scholasticism. He is considered the father of modern empiricism which stressed the inductive approach proceeding from particular facts to general theories to explain these facts.

Bacon's utopia was known as "Bensalem." It was an island in the southern hemisphere. The most important institution was the House of Salomon (also known as the College of Six Days' Works). The members of this college represented a scientific elite. They conducted numerous experiments including refrigerated caves, weather observation towers, and the creation of artificial foods and minerals. All disease was eliminated. There was a scientific intelligence service that garnered knowledge from other countries. Concerning marriage, Bacon was rather conservative. He did not condone premarital sex as did Campanella nor even premarital inspection as did More. The major question raised by Bacon's utopia is, "Are scientists the servants or saviors of the state?" The essence of democracy is that both the military and civilian experts (including scientists) should be accountable to politically elected officials who are in turn accountable to the people. As Churchill said, experts should be on tap, not on top. The problem with the increasing complexity of the world is that only the experts know what they are talking about and so it is difficult to hold them accountable. The sad thing is that the experts in the various fields cannot communicate with each other either.

Saint-Simon did not give us a precise formula for a utopia but like Bacon, did place great emphasis on technology. His major work was **The New Christianity** (1825). He is sometimes categorized as a utopian socialist although he was not as socialistic as people like Robert Owen. He did believe natural resources should be publicly owned but did not believe in absolute equality of distribution. There are two variants of the socialist formula. The first and purest is "From each according to his ability, to each according to his need." The second is, "From each according to his ability, to each according to his work." Saint-Simon believed in the latter. Both are contrasted to the capitalist formula which roughly says, "To each according to his ability to command others." According to Saint-Simon, in traditional social systems many people are useless. He raised the question as to what would happen if various members of the aristocracy mysteriously disappeared and concluded that it would make little difference to society. If, on the other hand, scientific and industrial geniuses disappeared society would collapse. He advocated, therefore, that government should be based on a three-fold separation of powers. There would be a House of Invention and a House of Examination to develop new ideas and to consider their practicability. Both houses would be staffed by scientists. There would be a House of Implementation to apply these ideas. This would be staffed by industrialists and managerial types. While there would be income differentials, Saint-Simon believed that the common ownership of resources would eliminate speculation and that the more rational use of resources would provide abundance for everyone.

One of the most elaborated utopias was described by Edward Bellamy in **Looking Backward** (1888). As a young man, Bellamy traveled in Europe and was depressed by the conditions he saw there. He became a social critic and reformist. One of his most delightful essays is "The Parable of the Watertank" in a book entitled Equality. This is about a group of entrepreneurs who build a watertank (the marketplace) and persuaded people to bring water for which they were paid one penny per pail. But when the people wanted to consume water they had to pay two pennies per pail. Eventually this led to a depression in which all suffered. Ultimately there was a revolution and the people assumed direct control over the watertank.

The hero of **Looking Backward** was Julian West He seemed to have had a Rip Van Winkle experience in which he fell asleep in a secret chamber of his basement and woke up 113 years later (actually it was simply a dream). In this dream, the process of concentration of industry had continued until finally, to correct the abuses of the great trusts, the government (The Great Trust) nationalized all industry. Everyone in the country became either a member or honorary member of the Industrial Army. This army bore certain resemblances to the corporate state. The economy was divided into ten departments or guilds, each representing a major industry. Heading each department was a lieutenant-general. The President of the United States was, in effect, the commanding general. Each department was structured somewhat like an army division into regiments, battalions, *etcetera*. All citizens, male and female, joined the army at age 21. For the first three years they were required to perform the more unpleasant tasks. After that they were given a choice of vocation insofar as was possible. At the age of 45 they retired. Since it was an army, members could not vote. Only the retired members had this right. The head of each department was elected by all the retired members of that department. When a vacancy occurred in the presidency, he was elected from the department heads by all voters in the country.

There were no wages but everyone received an equal allowance at the beginning of each year. It was argued that machinery had equalized everyone's productive capacity so that income differentials were not justified. People worked out of a sense of pride and usefulness rather than for economic gain. Women were liberated. Since they were economically independent, they could marry for love rather than for a meal ticket. Creativity was encouraged in that people who wrote books or created works of art could sell them. Such crimes as might be motivated by economic inequities had disappeared. The crimes which did occur were attributed to hereditary factors. Criminals were treated as diseased persons. There were no wars since the entire world was a loose confederation of national utopias. As one character states, "Who are the public enemies: Are they France, England, Germany, or hunger, cold, and nakedness?" Travel was permitted. Accounts could be transferred from country to country. Inventions such as radio, credit cards, and shopping centers were anticipated. Decorations were used for rewards rather than money. While this may seem absurd it is precisely what the military does.. In summary, Bellamy's utopia does seem a pleasant enough place. The most general criticism was that he achieved a mechanized equality at the expense of esthetics.

A final work in this category is **A Modern Utopia** (1905) by H.G. Wells. He represented perhaps one of the last of the universal men. (In the 20th century, it is almost impossible to be well versed in everything.) Wells was journalist, historian, scientist, novelist, and science-fiction writer. The **Outline of History** was one of the first attempts to write a truly world history. Prior to this book, most world histories ignored the oriental world. He was a student of Thomas Huxley, a famous biologist and the grandfather of Aldous

Huxley, also a utopian writer. In his many works, Wells ranges from extreme pessimism in **The Time Machine** (discussed in Chapter Six) to extreme optimism as in **Men Like Gods.**

A Modern Utopia does not have too much of a plot but is more a collection of ideas. Wells imagined himself on a planet identical to earth in another solar system. His utopia was a world state ruled by the Samurai. This was a meritocracy for which all were eligible provided they could pass an extremely rigorous examination and agreed to abide by a rigid code of ethics. They were required to lead a rather austere life and were denied the normal pleasures of life. Once a year they had to spend a week in the wilderness in a kind of survival test. Marriage was within the Samurai class to maintain excellence. People were divided into four classes: The Poietic, The Kinetic, the Dull, and the Base. The first three were roughly the equivalent of the three classes in Plato's society. The Samurai were generally from the Poietic class. The Base could be from any of the first three classes but generally were more selfish and egotistical.

Concerning economics, all property was owned by the world state and was leased to local authorities. Money and private property (as a means of expressing one's personality) did exist but everyone was assured of proper food, clothing, housing, and health care. Much of the labor was done by machinery. There was no discrimination against race or sex. The religion of utopia was humanistic with no doctrine of original sin. While there was considerable freedom, there was a system of mandatory registration of thumbprints. A central bureau in Paris maintained such prints for the entire world population. At the beginning of his work, Wells stated that his utopia was kinetic rather than static as are most utopias. Thus there were failures and crime did exist but rather than being executed or imprisoned, criminals were placed on isolated islands. One dystopian aspect of this society was the killing of all "deformed and monstrous and evilly diseased births." A totalitarian feature was the requirement for marriage. "It must occur only under certain obvious conditions, the contracting parties must be in healthy condition, free from specific transmissible taints, above a certain minimum age (women 21, men about 26), and sufficiently intelligent and energetic to have acquired a minimum education."

THE REJECTION OF TECHNOLOGY. The various utopian and dystopian works which reject technology may be divided into satirical and serious types. Among the satirists are Jonathan Swift, Samuel Butler, Edward Bulwer-Lytton, and Kurt Vonnegut.

Jonathan Swift was an Anglican church official but was disappointed by his failure in church politics. As a result, he became a very embittered man. His most famous work, **Gulliver's Travels** (1726), is often read as children's literature but contains a great deal of acidic social commentary. His hero, Lemuel Gulliver, has numerous adventures in Lilliput, Brobdingnab, Laputa, and in the country of Houyhnhnms. In the country of Lilliput (wee people), political factions divided over such serious issues as wearing high or low heels and the merits of cracking boiled eggs on the big or little end. A major feature of Brobdingnab (land of the giants) was that no law might be longer than twenty-two words. The sharpest satire, however, came in the account of Laputa. This was really a dystopia ruled by an elite which lived on a floating island. By manipulating this island the elite could either crush rebels or deny them sunlight. There was a royal society which engaged in ridiculous experiments such as building houses from the roof down or plowing fields by having pigs root up acorns placed there for that purpose. This is reminiscent of some of the experiments financed by the American National Science Foundation which do not make much more sense. While the floating island seems a bit absurd it is not quite so far-fetched in light of modern satellites. A more utopian society was the land of the Houyhnhnms. This was a country ruled by very rational horses (the name represents the horse's whinny). It is a rather anarchistic society in that the residents lived together in a kind of natural harmony. Since the horses were both rational and benevolent there was no need for extensive security precautions or for a welfare-state. There was an Assembly which issued exhortations rather than laws. There were two major flaws in this utopias. First was the absence of any feelings of love or other emotions. Second was the existence of the Yahoos who were half-human, half-ape. This reflected Swift's low opinion of his fellowman. The word has become an addition to our vocabulary. The theme of animal superiority over men occurs in the movie series, **Planet of the Apes.**

A less harsh satire on technological utopias was that of Samuel Butler in **Erewhon** (roughly "Nowhere" spelled backwards) written in 1872. Butler was the son of a clergyman but, like Swift, became disenchanted with organized religion. Much of his work was a satire on religion. Erewhon seems to have been located in the northern half of New Zealand. It was divided by a mountain range from the known inhabitants. The hero discovered the place after getting lost in the mountains. This was an agrarian utopia. Politically it was a monarchy, economically it was a capitalist system. Persons who acquired money were greatly revered.

There were a number of interesting features in this utopia. One of the most important was the rejection of technology. It was feared that machines would develop consciousness and rule men. Just how far-fetched is this? Will computers in the future be able to think? Already it is possible for chess-playing computer programmers to write programs for computers that will play better chess than they do. In more subtle ways machines do dominate us. More and more we arrange our lives so everything can be fit into a computer or we slave to support our "holy cars" and then laugh at the Indians and their "holy cows." A second stab was directed at the utopian stress on reason. Butler points out that rationality pushed to extremes becomes irrationality. At one point in time, the Erewhonians became vegetarians because they believed animals had the right to life just as humans. Only animals who died or who "committed suicide" could be eaten. This led to a mysterious increase in animal suicides! The principle of rights was then applied to vegetables. Only those which had decayed could be eaten. Eventually a wise man revealed the absurdity of it all, reciting the following ditty to guide their actions:

> He who sins aught sins more than he ought,
> But he who sins naught has much to be taught,
> Beat or be beaten, eat or be eaten,
> Be killed or kill, do as you will.

Another aspect of this satire were Colleges of Unreason with professorships of Inconsistency and Evasion and in which hypothetics was taught. "To imagine a set of utterly strange and impossible contingencies, and require the youths to give intelligent answers to the questions that arise therefrom, is reckoned the fittest conceivable way of preparing them for the actual conduct of their affairs in after life." This is really not so different from the "new math." Our politicians would be well qualified for the professorships of Inconsistency and Evasion! A third feature had to do with the world of the unborn. The Erewhonians believed that there were spirits dwelling around us who came here from other planets. They wanted to become human. The only way they could achieve this was to agree to be born as helpless infants and run the risk of having stupid parents. This would seem to be a satire on the person who is so anxious to get to heaven that he fails to enjoy this life. Also a satire on religion were "musical banks." These were banks in which people kept accounts which had no negotiable value. Butler seemed to believe that religious faith has no practical use in this world. Finally, there was the question of crime and disease. Crime was treated as a disease, disease as a crime. Today we do the former when we attempt to rehabilitate criminals and the latter in our treatment of the elderly indigent in disgracefully run nursing homes. It is these very oddities which makes Butler's work such delightful reading.

With **The Coming Race** (1871) of Edward Bulwer-Lytton, utopian literature took a rather sharp turn in the direction of science fiction. The hero of this work was exploring an abandoned mine-shaft which led him into a subterranean utopia. A race of people known as the Vrilya Confederation had created a fantastic world in huge caverns below the surface of the each. They had a rather angelic appearance, having developed removable wings by means of which they were able to fly. A major achievement was the discovery of a mysterious power called Vril. It manifested itself in both psychic and physical forms. As a psychic power it could be used to exercise control over mind and body (both animal and vegetable). As a physical power it would seem to parallel modern-day laser beams. This power was possessed by all. Although any person had the power to annihilate any other person, he never did so for fear of retaliation. In this way, the Vrilya Confederation had eliminated the problem of both internal and external violence. It should be noted that Bulwer-Lytton lived in the later half of the 19th century and despaired at the futility of arms races. His discussion of Vril power was a rather obvious satire on man's attempt to avoid war by constantly preparing for it. This satire becomes even more pointed in light of the contemporary nuclear proliferation. As Churchill stated, "We are wandering on the brink of hell."

This utopia bears several resemblances to Bacon's **New Atlantis**. First, it was not a socialistic community. Property and money did exist but they did not confer special privilege. There were no extreme disparities of wealth, however, since science had made an abundant life available to all. Second, scientific development took place under the direction of a College of Sages, analogous to the House of Salomon. In this case, however, it was staffed by women. Here the author was satirizing the Victorian contempt for feminine intellectual power. Third, it was an extremely static utopia. The people led very serene lives with no desire for wealth or power. The ruler of this utopia was Tur, a benevolent despot. It was not, however, a police state. There were no police or armies since Vril power rendered them unnecessary. Also, since science had provided affluence for all, there was no need for an elaborate welfare state. It might be ironically described as a kind of authoritarian anarchy.

While Bulwer-Lytton described a highly technological society, his work is included in the anti-technological category because of his

satire of Vril power. In a similar way, Kurt Vonnegut satirizes
technology by describing a highly automated society. In **Player
Piano** (1952), he pictures the United States at some time in the
future in which virtually all meaningful jobs have been eliminated
by automation. The only people with any significant work are the
engineers who design and maintain the computers. We may already
be much closer to this reality than we think. One of the problems
with this is that computers do not buy things. The market for
material goods will begin to dry up. People automated out of jobs
will have to be placed on welfare. The entire process of production
and distribution becomes much more politicized. In this dystopia,
people automated out of jobs are either in the Army or in the
Reconstruction and Reclamation Corps (Reeks and Wrecks).

The American political system superficially looks the same but the
politicians perform only ceremonial functions. In a rather significant
passage one of the characters of the novel "stared at President
Jonathan Lynn and imagined with horror what the country must
have been like when, as today, any damn fool little American boy
might grow up to be President, but when the President had to
actually run the country." The real power is exercised by the
engineers but even they seem helpless in the face of their creature.
The Big Brother of 1984 (discussed in Chapter Six) has been
replaced by EPICAC XIV, a giant computer. Vonnegut points out
that the greatest need is the need to be needed. In a moving passage
a character says, "Now the machines take all the dangerous jobs, and
the dumb bastards just get tucked away...and there's nothing for
them to do but set there and kind of hope for a big fire where maybe
they can run into a burning building...and run out with a baby in
their arms. Or maybe hope...for another war." In the final chapter

there is a revolution in which the masses destroy the machines (somewhat similar to the Luddite movement of the 19th century) but in the very last scene, people are digging through the rubble trying to reconstruct the machines.

So far in this chapter, emphasis has been on the satirizing of technology. Attention will now be paid to more serious discussions of agrarian societies. One of these is described by William Morris in **News from Nowhere** (1890). As a young man, Morris was engaged in the interior decoration business; as an older man he became a socialist. These two themes are united in a rather pleasing esthetic socialistic utopia. The narrator dreams that he is living in London some time in the distant future. Although it is a futuristic society in chronological terms, it resembles 14th century England. He discovers that there had been a struggle between the bourgeoisie and the proletariat but instead of a victory by the latter as Marx predicted, the two groups agreed that their salvation lay in abandoning industrialism. As one character says, "England was once a country of clearings among the woods and wastes, with a few towns interspersed, which were fortresses for the feudal army, markets for the folk, gathering places for the craftsmen. It then became a country of huge and foul workshops and fouler gambling dens, surrounded by an ill-kept, poverty-stricken farm, polluted by the masters of the work-shops. It is now a garden, where nothing is wasted and nothing is spoilt, with the necessary dwellings, sheds, and workshops scattered up and down the country, all trim and neat and pretty." This utopia combines the best principles of esthetic beauty with those of economic efficiency and justice.

People now lived in a simple agrarian society. All property was publicly owned. People worked not for economic motives but as an expression of creativity. They lived in very pleasant houses and wore simple but attractive clothing. Since there was no crime or poverty there was no need for government. Manure was stored in the former parliament buildings! Concerning the absence of labor-saving machines, one character states labor is saved "in order that it might be expended, I will say wasted, on another, probably useless, piece of work. Friends, all their devices for cheapening labor simply resulted in increasing the burden of labor."

An agrarian utopia which totally rejected technology was **Islandia** (1942) by Austin Wright. As an attorney and professor law, he apparently wrote this novel more as a means of escape than for publication. It was not published until after his untimely death in an auto accident. The country of Islandia was on the continent of Karain (similar to Australia) in the southern hemisphere. It had a semi-feudal society in which a few families owned most of the land. They treated their tenants kindly and reasonably and so everyone seemed happy enough. There was, however, a modernizing faction that did want to import modern technology. The traditionalists resisted this. They argued that progress only created other inequities. Perhaps one of the most important concepts in the book is the way in which love was defined. There were four types of love: (1) *amia*, a Platonic love of friend for friend; (2) *apia*, passionate love but not for a lengthy duration; (3) *ania*, the deeper love needed for a lifetime commitment; and (4) *alia*, or love of place. This latter love of place explained much of the conservatism in this society. People were reluctant to leave the place in which they were born because their personality was so deeply rooted there. Furthermore, they did not want to change this place in any way for then it was no longer the same place. We all have this feeling about some cherished place of our childhood and die a little when some building is razed or tree cut down.

A less radical rejection of technology is Huxley's **Island** (1962). This book was written a generation after his **Brave New World** and represents a much more attractive picture of the future. It was an agrarian utopia located on an island in the south Seas. The formal ruler was a constitutional monarch. There was a parliament to which members were elected from both territorial districts as well as from vocational and professional groups. Although not socialistic, most enterprises were of a cooperative nature. As in Morris' utopia, work served more as a means to express oneself than to acquire money. It was a means of enlightenment. Labor rotation was used. Technology was used selectively for medical purposes and to increase food production. Groups of families (15 to 25) made up Mutual Adoption Clubs. By permitting children to occasionally live with other families within the club, both children and parents were allowed freedom from each other. The Islanders also practiced a yoga of love somewhat similar to the male continence of the Oneida community (discussed in Chapter Four).

The educational system stressed both individual and group values. Hypnosis and a mescaline-like drug called Moksha were used to help Islanders achieve the ultimate consciousness. One feature of the modern world since the beginnings of the scientific revolution has been to see man in only one dimension, the rational. The islanders would have agreed with William Blake in his poem:

> Now I a four-fold vision see,
> and a four-fold vision is given to me;
> 'Tis four-fold in my supreme delight
> and threefold in soft Beulah's night.
> And twofold always. May God us keep
> from single vision and Newton's sleep.

He saw man in four dimensions: (1) rational, (2) emotional, (3) psychic, and (4) spiritual. The Islanders would surely agree with this.

▼

CHAPTER FOUR

THE DREAM SURVEYED: UTOPIA AND ECONOMICS

UTOPIAN CAPITALISM. Most utopists are socialists, believing that human conflicts are usually economic in nature and can be eliminated only by abolishing private property. Capitalists believe man is not altruistic enough to make the sacrifices socialism requires. Ayn Rand believed that not only was sacrifice bad in that it destroyed the initiative of the person for whom it was made, but that selfishness was a positive good.

She was born in Russia and lived through the Bolshevik Revolution. The excesses of the revolution disenchanted her with socialism. Her writings are also influenced by an early infatuation with Nietzsche, the German philosopher who believed that people were divided into active (Dionysian) and passive (Apollonian) types. He took these terms from the Greek gods of revelry and reason, respectively. The active minority are driven by an inner will to power. These people are not bound by the standards codes of morality. They ultimately become the elite that dominates society. All of Rand's heroes, such as John Galt in **Atlas Shrugged**, are Nietzschean types.

Before taking a brief look at this work, the similarities of Rand's thought to that of Adam Smith and Herbert Spencer should be noted. In 1776, Adam Smith in **The Wealth of Nations** observed that the real wealth of a nation lay not in its gold or silver reserves but in its agricultural and industrial productivity. The latter depended on division of labor. Individuals and nations would both profit if they specialized in some endeavor thus becoming more efficient. This would necessitate an elaborate system for the exchange of goods and services. In such a system, emphasis could be placed either on centralized government planning agencies or on a free market. Smith opted for the latter. Thus he believed in *laissez-faire* government; that is, one that does not interfere with the business world except perhaps to protect strategic industries by a high tariff. Also believing in *laissez-faire* government but for different reasons was Herbert Spencer. An evolutionist, Spencer believed in the survival of the fittest and in the genetic transmission of acquired characteristics. He opposed socialist or welfare states because by helping the incompetent to survive they would interfere with the natural selection process.

In the last chapter, mention was made of Saint-Simon's observation that the disappearance of scientific and industrial leaders would cause economic chaos. This is the plot of **Atlas Shrugged** (1957). The entire world, except the United States, is made up of Socialist

People's Republics. Even in the United States attempts were being made to socialize the country. Among other things, an Equalization of Opportunity Act was passed. Under the provisions of this act, companies able to produce more efficiently than their competitors were not permitted to undersell them. Because of this and other stifling legislation, numerous scientists and businessmen led by John Galt mysteriously disappeared. By dropping out they hoped to show the proponents of socialism that it would not work because it discouraged the individual entrepreneur, the man who "puts it all together." They withdrew to a small mountain valley in Colorado where they created their own utopia. One of their members becomes a pirate who believed he was merely righting wrongs by taking back from governments what the latter had confiscated from private enterprise. "I'm after a man whom, I want to destroy," he says. "It is said that he (Robin Hood) fought against the looting rulers and returned the loot to those who had been robbed, but that is not the meaning of the legend which has survived. He is remembered, not as a champion of property, but as a champion of need, not as a defender of the robbed, but as a provider of the poor…He became a justification for every mediocrity who unable to make his own living, has demanded the power to dispose of the property of his betters, by proclaiming his willingness to devote his life to his inferiors at the price of robbing his superiors."

In another famous passage, the hero John Galt challenges both the Christian doctrine of original sin and its secularized version. Marx, for example, believed that natural man was altruistic but had fallen into a "sinful" acquisitive state. "What is the nature of the guilt your teachers call his Original Sin? What are the evils man acquired when he fell from a state they consider perfection? Their myth declares that he ate the fruit of the tree of knowledge; he acquired a mind and became a rational being. It was the knowledge of good and evil; he became a moral being. He was sentenced to earn his bread by his labor; he became a productive being. He was sentenced to experience desire; he acquired the capacity of sexual enjoyment. The evil for which they damn him are reason, morality, creativeness, joy, all the cardinal virtues of his existence. It is not his vices that their myth of man's fall is designed to explain and condemn, it is not his errors that they hold as his guilt, but the essence of his nature as a man. Whatever he was; that robot in the Garden of Eden, who existed without mind, without values, without labor, without love; he was not man."

A much less philosophical work is **Alpaca** (1960) by H.L. Hunt, the famous Texas oilman. Alpaca is a mythical country in South America. It is very much a capitalistic utopia. Its constitution states that "the Government shall conduct its affairs to compete as little as possible with private industry." No one should pay more than 25 percent of his income in taxes. People who are among the top half of the taxpayers and/or who refuse government salaries or retirement payments are accorded additional votes. Bureaucracy is very much feared. Government agencies are to be annually reviewed and if they cannot justify their existence shall be abolished. Laws automatically expire at the end of twelve years unless reenacted thirty days before their expiration. Civil servants accused of treasonable or illegal activities are to be suspended from service until they have proven their innocence.

The political structure of Alpaca is based on the collegial system of Switzerland. There are essentially four branches of government;

executive, legislative, judicial, and military. The members of each branch are elected by an electoral college in turn elected by the voters. The executive branch consists of a triumvirate. Collegial executives of this nature are generally weaker than single-headed executives since a committee can never act as quickly as one person. The triumvirate is further weakened by subordination to a National Policy Committee consisting of the Chairman of the Triumvirate, the Chief Justice, and the Chairman of the Legislative Veto Board (one of the two houses of the legislative branch). Government was to be based on a continuing debate between a Liberal and a Constructive party. The first stressed socialistic and paternalistic government; the second emphasized private property rights, the profit motive and individual initiative.

To understand Hunt's emphasis on decentralized power it is necessary to compare two opposing views of government. The socialist thinks that government is a capitalist conspiracy; the capitalist sees it as a socialist conspiracy. The fear of creeping socialism was at the root of Hunt's desire for decentralized government. Liberal and socialist critics of Hunt would see his ideas rendering government impotent and permitting the capitalists to be the real "government" of the country. Rather oddly, however, some of Hunt's themes are now being adopted by liberals. In the aftermath of Watergate, for example, liberals want to reduce the power of the presidency and increase the powers of congress. Also, a number of state legislatures are experimenting with "sunset " laws that do expire after a given time unless re-legislated.

UTOPIAN SOCIALISM. While the great majority of both fictional and experimental utopias are socialistic, the term "utopian socialism" has been used in a rather specific way to refer to a group of socialists in the 18th and 19th centuries who advocated the creation of small, voluntary, socialistic communities. They hoped that by setting a good example they would set in motion an irreversible trend that would culminate in a worldwide confederation of such communities. They did not call themselves utopian socialists. As was noted earlier, the term was applied to them by Marx and Engels who believed such a program to promote socialism was impractical. In exploring this category of utopian thought, a distinction will be made between the secular European models and the more religious American types.

The European socialists were concerned with three very specific problems arising out of the industrial revolution. The first of these involved the gross inequities of wealth. Capitalists were accumulating huge fortunes at one end of the spectrum while workers labored for wage slavery and under sweatshop conditions at the other end. The second problem was the boom-bust cycle frequently occurring in industrial economies. In some cases, this was caused by the lack of purchasing power resulting from the extremely low wages paid the workers. A third problem was that of over-specialization of labor. While a good deal of specialization is necessary to make possible an industrial economy, it can reach a point of diminishing returns. Assembly-line methods, for example, forcing workers to repeat some simple routine over and over again have a dehumanizing effect on the workers. The latter become, in effect, human robots. Both their morale and efficiency decline drastically.

The utopian socialists suggested the creation of small relatively self-contained communities of perhaps 1500 to 2000 people living on four or five thousand acres of land. These communities were communally owned thus resolving the problem of inequity. They would engage in both agricultural and industrial enterprises. Being able to produce most of their food and a good part of their other needs, they were somewhat insulated from the above-mentioned boom-bust cycle. In many of these communities they would follow More's example of rotation of labor thus reducing the element of boredom.

Two of the most famous proponents of such communities were Robert Owen in Britain and Charles Fourier in France. Owen was a self-made millionaire with a social conscience. He created one community in New Lanark, Scotland which he ran along rather autocratic lines. He later established a larger community in New Harmony, Indiana which was run more democratically. This latter community eventually collapsed due to internal conflicts. Owen believed that man could be shaped by his environment. By creating communitarian life that encouraged a spirit of altruism, he believed people would indeed be altruistic. He called his communities Parallelograms as there was a to be an inner rectangle consisting of residence and light industry and an outer rectangle made up of an agricultural green belt. His opponents called them Parallelograms of Poverty since they believed socialism to be a system in which everyone tried to live at the expense of everyone else.

Charles Fourier was not as optimistic about changing man's nature. His communities (called Phalanstaries) were essentially joint-stock companies. Five-twelfths of such income was divided on the basis of equal pay for all except that unpleasant work did receive somewhat higher pay. Four-twelfths was divided among the investors in the community in proportion to their investment. Here Fourier seems to have been more Calvinist than Marxist. (The Calvinists believed that capital was accumulated by thrift; Marxists believed it was accumulated by theft, by the capitalist underpaying workers and overcharging customers.) Three-twelfths was divided on the basis of natural talents or acquired skills. Fourier believed, in other words, that material and individual incentives must be held out to induce people to save the necessary capital to establish such communities and to take the time and effort to acquire the needed technical skills.

Although he did not draw up specific designs for utopia, Rousseau was similar to Owen and Fourier in that he also advocated small, socialistic communities. Smallness, for Rousseau, was necessary for still another purpose. He believed that public policy should rest on the general will of the body politic; that is, what everyone had in common. Determining this general will required two things. All citizens should participate directly in making decisions. If their input was filtered through elected representatives there was a danger of distortion. Second, votes would not be taken. Such vote could only determine the general will of the majority. Instead, discussions would ideally continue until unanimity was reached. This is very impractical which, according to More's definition, would make it all the more utopian! In practice, countries which have claimed to base policy on the general will have generally been authoritarian in nature. Napoleon, Hitler, and DeGaulle did it though the use of referendums which they manipulated to get the desired result. The black leaders of former French colonies in Africa who were exposed to Rousseau's writings in their education in Paris have shaped the general will through the one-party state.

A fictional utopia that did seem to be based on the general will concept was that described by Etienne Cabet in **Voyage to Icaria** (1840). This was an ideal state isolated from the rest of the world by mountains on the north and south, a river at the east, and the sea at the west. He probably had the area west of the Mississippi River in mind. This state had been created by a dictator, Icar, who seemed modeled after Napoleon. It was a people's democracy in which there was a government elected by and accountable to the people. There was also, however, a "committee of experts" which prepared various plans and regulations for submission to the legislature. In reality, it seems to have been a technocracy since the recommendations of the experts were usually accepted. The capital city was somewhat reminiscent of Amaurot with its concern for symmetry. It was located on a circular island in the middle of a river. All streets ran parallel to each other. This presents the eternal problem of squaring the circle! In each quarter there was a hospital, a school, a temple, shops, public places, and monuments.

For the most part, life was pleasant enough. Workdays were not too long, most disagreeable work was done by machines, retirement was permitted at 65 for men and 50 for women. In some ways, however, it resembled the totalitarian regimes of the 20th century. Life was minutely regulated including the time of rising and retiring, diet, clothing, *etcetera*. Architecture was of the grandiose type similar to that of Nazi Germany and Fascist Italy. The image of the dead dictator was prominently displayed in public (like Orwell's Big Brother). It is also very reminiscent of Mao Zedung's "empire of blue ants" in the 1950s and 1960s. As in Mao's China, the people had been subtly conditioned so that this regimentation was the "general will" of the people. In other ways it is an exaggerated picture of

France which is a democracy but with a high degree of government
regulation.

Cabet was not just a dreamer. He attempted to create such a
community in the United States. A tract of land was bought in Texas
but it consisted of alternate sections of land in a checkerboard
fashion. This made impossible the creation of a compact, contiguous
community. The colony then moved to Iowa. Under-capitalization
and extensive discord among the membership led to the failure of
the experiment.

In the United States, there were many socialistic communities in the
18th and 19th centuries. Most were religious in nature having been
inspired by the 16th century Anabaptists who took their inspiration
in turn from the first-century Christian communes discussed in **Acts
4**. It is rather interesting to note that a book about these
communities, **Communistic Societies of the United States** (1875)
by Charles Nordhoff, was not considered controversial. Only since
the 1917 Russian Revolution has socialism become a bad word in
the United States.

Only a few of these communities can be mentioned here. They were
all rather similar in their economic arrangements but did differ
rather sharply in their views of sex. The most conservative were the
Shaker communities. They began as an offshoot of the Quakers.
Among their beliefs was the notion of the bisexual nature of God.
Just as God had been incarnate in the male form in Christ, so they
believed God had been incarnate in the female form in the person
of one Ann Lee born in Manchester, England in the 18th century.
With her birth, the Shakers believed the millennium had begun.

They advocated, therefore, only brotherly and sisterly rather than sexual love. The communities maintained their existence by recruiting members from the outside world. Today there are only two communities left, one in Sabbath Day Lake, Maine and one in Canterbury, New Hampshire. Also ascetic but not to the point of celibacy, was the Amana community in Iowa. Marriages were permitted but sex was considered to be only for procreative purposes. Men and women sat at separate tables in the dining halls and on separate sides in church. Their asceticism did not, however, apply to food as they ate rather large quantities. In the early 1930s, the Amana community was incorporated as a joint-stock company. Today it is the producer of the famous Amana radar ovens.

Still less conservative on the question of sex were the Mormons who practiced polygamy. As a result they were persecuted throughout the middle west and finally migrated to Utah. There they created a utopia out of the desert. Initially the Mormons practiced what might be called "church socialism" in that many businesses were owned by the church. This is not so true today. When Utah applied for statehood, the Mormons agreed to put a clause into the state constitution prohibiting polygamy. In theory, that clause could be repealed since the United States constitution leaves the regulation of marriage in the hands of state governments.

The most liberal of the religious communities regarding sex was the Oneida community founded by Alfred Noyes. The Oneidans were called Perfectionists. They believed the Second Coming of Christ had taken place in the year 70 and like the Shakers they were millennialists. The two unique features of Oneida were complex marriage and male continence. Any man and women could by mutual consent begin and end a sexual relationship whenever they so desired. For them, more orthodox marriages were really just property arrangements. Male continence was the term used for the withdrawal method of birth control. It apparently was fairly successful as there were few unplanned pregnancies. Like Amana, the Oneida community was later converted into a private corporation.

A final community to be discussed was that of Brook Farm. This was founded by a mixture of Unitarians and Transcendentalists. The former denied the existence of the Trinity. The later should be called Immanentalists since they really seemed to believe that God, or the divine spark, was immanent in man. While most of the other communities earned cash income by selling agricultural or industrial products, Brook Farm maintained itself by running several schools. The community sadly ended when the buildings burned down. A novel, **The Blithedale Romance** (1852) by Nathaniel Hawthorne, was about Brook Farm.

In general, the secular communities were less successful than the religious ones. There were many reasons for their failures. First, they existed in an hostile environment. The surrounding communities usually considered the members of these groups to be eccentric at best and subversive at worst. Second, they were undercapitalized. Third, they often had recruitment problems. They were successful in attracting intellectuals who disliked the hard physical labor and "dropout" types who were looking for a free ride. They were less successful in attracting "blue-collar" types without which a viable economic community could not be maintained. It seems not too unfair to say that members of this latter group have less social conscience than intellectuals do (or at least claim to have). Finally, while socialists often claim that all conflict disappears with private property, this simply is not so. Members of these communities found many other things about which to argue. The religious communities, on the other hand, were more successful since their members were motivated by a greater spirit of altruism. But as these communities became more secular, they too failed.

MIXED VARIETIES. In the treatment of socialistic and capitalistic utopias, at least two did not fall clearly into either category, those of Saint-Simon and Fourier. Another example of the mixed variety was **Freeland** (1890) by Theodor Hertzka. An Austrian economist, Hertzka attempted to found a community in East Africa but ran into opposition from the colonial powers. His utopia was based on five principles: (1) public ownership of all resources as advocated by Saint-Simon, (2) the maximum freedom for each person that was compatible with a similar freedom for others, (3) universal suffrage, (4) public support for the disabled and poor, and (5) both the executive and legislative branches of government were to be divided into specialized departments or committees. Today, much of this program would no longer be considered utopian but simply taken for granted.

One other example of a mixed utopia was that described by Colonel Edward House in **Philip Dru: Administrator** (1912). The author is perhaps more interesting than the book. House was a close advisor to President Wilson. Like many utopian books, it is not great literature. It often reads like a soap opera.

Philip Dru, a young idealistic army officer, is disgusted by the corruption he sees in the United States. He raises a private army and with superior tactics defeats the national government forces. After capturing Washington he proclaimed himself the Administrator of the Republic. One of his first tasks was to reorganize the judiciary. The number of courts was reduced by the expedient of forbidding lawyers to bring frivolous cases to court (once again the anti-lawyer bias). Judges were forced to retire at age 70. The power to declare laws unconstitutional was taken away from the courts (both House and Wilson were proponents of parliamentary government which generally does not have judicial review power since it is based on the principle of legislative supremacy). A new and simplified code of laws was prepared. A second major task was tax reform. Unimproved land or land lying idle was taxed at a higher rate than improved land and land in production. A graduated income tax was adopted (the book was written before the adoption of the 16th Amendment which first made such taxes constitutional). A third step was to enact a Federal Incorporation Act. Labor was to have at least one representative on the board of directors and to share in the profits. It in turn gave up the right to strike and agreed to submit all grievances to arbitration. A fourth step was to extend suffrage to all. Finally, a new constitution was drawn up creating a parliamentary form of government. In summary, the capitalistic system was permitted to exist but under the supervision of a more highly centralized government that was the guardian of the public interest rather than of the special interests. Having achieved his reforms, our hero resigns as Administrator and sails off into the sunset on his yacht with his bride!

CHAPTER FIVE

THE DREAM SURVEYED: UTOPIA AND TERRITORY

MINITOPIA. So far, this discussion of utopias has been confined to communities. We may each of us have our own private utopia such as a corner in the house where we have all of our books or a favorite walk in the woods. At some time, we have all been tempted to do the Walden scene. Thoreau gives his reason for seeking out such a life. "I went to the woods because I wished to live deliberately, to front only the essential facts of life and see if I could not learn what it had to teach, and not, when I came to die, discover that I had not lived. I wanted to…drive life into a corner, and reduce it to its lowest terms, and, if it proved to be mean, why then to get the whole and genuine meanness out of it, and publish its meanness to the world; or, if it were sublime, to know it by experience…"

Another type of such literature is represented by **Robinson Crusoe** (1719) by Daniel Defoe and **Swiss Family Robinson** (1820) by Johann Wyss. We all have our "Robinsonade" moments when we wish to escape from the world. Were we actually shipwrecked we would feel utter despair. Both books are examples of how a man or family created a kind of utopia out of a bad situation. The movie **Man Friday** gives a rather dystopian view of this experience. According to a March 22, 1976 Newsweek review, "Crusoe, who has spent twelve years in shipwrecked solitude on a tropical island, is bent on preserving the standards of Christianity and the British Empire. He has built a jungle fortress in which he solemnly reads the Bible, salutes a tattered Union Jack and observes the ritual tea time. But beneath his civilized manner is an uncivil heart. When Friday, intelligent but illiterate, comes ashore from a neighboring island, Crusoe enslaves him. Bearing the white man's burden, he sets out to instill in Friday the value of money, sportsmanship, fear of God, and above all, unquestioning obedience to a rigid class system. While Crusoe hammers away at his servant, Friday attempts to teach him about sharing, living and brotherhood. The arrogant Crusoe is uneducable, blinded by adherence to a corrupt code of ethics. When Friday finally challenges him and rebels against his bondage, Crusoe goes bananas."

A rather frivolous example of this story was presented in the television series, **Gilligan's Island.** It was about the owner of a yacht and his assistant who were shipwrecked with five passengers. While on the whole it was a rather stupid program, there were some interesting utopian themes. Among the five passengers were a millionaire and his wife pictured as complete and total parasites. (Even Marx saw the capitalist as serving a useful function.) On the other extreme was the professor who was capable of anything from rigging a derrick to digging a well, a vote again for technology and against parasitic wealth.

A much grimmer experience was pictured in **Lord of the Flies** (1954) by William Golding. It is about a group of young English schoolboys who while being evacuated from home in war mysteriously survived a plane crash on a tropical island. All remnants of the crash were washed away to sea and so, unlike Robinson Crusoe, the boys were left completely to their own resources. Golding has a very pessimistic view of human nature. The boys degenerate to savages in the worst sense of the word. Contrary to a favorable utopian theme that if man frees himself from corrupt institutions he can create the perfect society, these boys created a literal hell.

MIDITOPIA. Most of the utopias studied so far would qualify as "miditopias." Two more examples worth considering are the Israeli kibbutzim and the Shangri-La of James Hilton. The origins of the kibbutz go back to the early days of the Zionist movement. The first kibbutzim were created in Palestine in the early 20th century, predating even the British mandate. They represent a small scale direct democracy. Whereas most organizatons are dominated by an elite, the governing body of the kibbutz is a general assembly based on a fusion of powers (no separation into executive, legislative, and judicial branches). While there are no institutional restraints on sex, it is not taken lightly. Children are reared in nurseries which in this case leads to early maturity. There is a generational problem. Compared to the first generation, the second (1) sees itself as a home rather than as a social experiment, as an emotional rather than a cognitive experience, (2) stresses the importance of persons over values, (3) emphasizes human rather than institutional factors, (4) is more individualist than collectivist, and (5) is less willing to accept austerity. Despite these differences (which are illustrated much more fully by Melford Spiro in **Kibbutz: Venture in Utopia**), the second generation, although often moving to another locale, does continue in the kibbutz tradition.

A delightful miditopia was Shangri-La described in **Lost Horizon** (1933) by James Hilton. This utopia was located high in the Himalayas in a valley sheltered by the mountains and so had an ideal climate. Due to this climate and the development of an unnamed drug, the lamas lived to be more than 200 years old. Little mention was made of the social and economic arrangements but no one seemed to be lacking the necessities of life. There was contact with the outside world and such modern items as bathroom fixtures had been imported. Hunza, a small protectorate of Pakistan, may have been the model for Shangri-La. It is sometimes described as a utopia because of its natural, unhurried, stress-free life. The inhabitants are noted for their longevity although accurate records are not kept. Hunza is being corrupted by the outside world. Sugar has been imported leading to cavities and goiters are beginning to appear now that white salt is replacing the brownish variety previously used.

MAXITOPIAS. Lewis Mumford, in **The Story of Utopias**, suggests one type of utopia is the Countryhouse. By this he means that wealthy people can afford to create their own private utopias. The Countryhouse is somewhat reminiscent of Rabelais' Abbey of Theleme with the emphasis on a life of ease. But the Countryhouses of the 19th century were not possible without the Coketowns; that is, the factory workers whose exploitation filled the corporate coffers. As one of G.B, Shaw's characters in **Major Barbara** says, "What kep' us poor? Keepin' you rich!" Marx believed that a horizontal organization of the Coketowns of the world would finally force the capitulation of the Countryhouses. What Mumford points out is that the National Utopia represents a vertical combination of Countryhouse and Coketown in each country. Coketown was convinced that it has less to fear from Countryhouse than from other Coketowns. Also, as Coketown has prospered it has emulated the Countryhouse. It may be cookout units instead of fireplaces and campers instead of cabins but the value system is essentially the same.

Having looked at the National Utopia in general, some mention will now be made of specific examples. Each of the three major powers of the world today (the United States, the Soviet Union, and Communist China) all see themselves in some way as utopias. In this country, our utopian perception of ourselves began with the Mayflower. As John Winthrop state, "We shall be as a City upon a Hill, the eyes of all people are upon us so that if we shall deal falsely with our God in this work and so cause Him to withdraw His present help from us, we shall be made a story and byword through the world."

In many ways, the United States is the most successful utopia on earth. More people have enjoyed greater political freedom and economic prosperity than anywhere on earth. But it could have been better. We have wasted our resources, corrupted our institutions, discriminated against our minorities. What went wrong? In his novel **The Farm** (1933), Louis Bromfield gives at least one answer. The owner of the farm is Jamie Ferguson who has created his own utopia, a Jeffersonian agrarian type. He prides himself that he raises practically everything he eats. But eventually the farm is swallowed up by the city. In the beginning chapter, Jamie's father-in-law, who had served as a colonel during the War of 1812, is going to Ohio to take possession of a land grant which was his reward for military service. Stopping overnight in a tavern, he has a long discussion with a Jesuit priest on his way to the Southwest. The colonel describes his dream of a simple agrarian republic such as Jefferson desired. As they speak, a peddler enters the inn and tries to sell them his wares. In a moving passage at the end of the book the author says, "But in the end the peddler won. After old Jamie came to live in the gray house in Town and his active days were over, he had spent hundreds of hours among newspapers and books, trying to understand all that which had happened so quickly about him, and out of these hours arose the only vindictiveness he ever knew in all his long life. It was directed toward the peddler, for he came to believe that it was New England which corrupted the democracy, the New England which long ago talked of a king and worried over titles and precedence, the New England which swindled the Revolutionary veterans and whose clergy preached privilege from their pulpits and soiled their cloth with obscene abuse of Jefferson. I think he always understood the peculiar vulgarity of New England, which to him was the vulgarity of a peddler grown rich in ways which were none too scrupulous. He was no enemy of the Puritan for he was himself Calvinistic to the end of his days. Puritanism at its best made a strong people and a good life, but Puritanism at its worst was tainted by the ideals of the shopkeeper....For old Jamie it was not Puritanism which had corrupted the Republic, but business (for) with Hamilton all the trouble had begun. The roots of the corruption lays in his teachings, that the government should be not in the hands of democrats or aristocrats but of plutocrats. Out of the beliefs and teachings of Hamilton had come the decay he had seen slowly paralyzing the government during his lifetime. He had seen a republic, a democracy, come to be run as a business, an affair of shopkeepers and money-changers, who paid out money upon which they expected returns in laws and tariffs and land grants. He had come to see American citizens look upon such bargains calmly and without indignation, protest or complaint....In the Town cemetery old Jamie had a simple granite headstone with the dates of his birth and death. There was no epitaph, but if there had been one it would have been brief and simple—'Here lies a good citizen.' If there had been more like him, the history of the United States since the Civil War would have been different."

One of the most utopian visions ever dreamed was that of Karl Marx. For Marx, the coming of utopia was inevitable, the final culmination of a dialectical process in history. This idea was borrowed from Hegel who also had a rather utopian view of history. For Hegel, the despotism of the orient (thesis) and the anarchy of the Greek city-state system (antithesis) were resolved in the disciplined democracy of modern Prussia (synthesis). Democracy was doing what we ought to do under the guidance of the state and not doing what we want to do with the permission of the state. Marx applied this dialectical process to economics. In the first stage of history there was a feudal synthesis between the freedom of primitive communism and the slavery which followed. In the second stage, there was a capitalist synthesis between land (feudal lords) and money (merchant lords). In the final stage, there was a communist synthesis between the owners (bourgeoisie) and the workers (proletariat) resulting in a classless society. More specifically, when the exploited workers overthrew the capitalist class in revolution they would create a "dictatorship of the proletariat." For Marx, this was not really a dictatorship but a workers' democracy. Eventually the revolution would spread to other countries, all capitalist regimes would be overthrown, and then states would wither sway since their only function had been to protect property rights. Thus Marx envisaged a worldwide socialist, classless utopia in which all lived happily ever after in a natural harmony.

The scenario did not unfold in this way for two major reasons. First, contrary to Marx's expectations, the revolution occurred first in Russia instead of in England or Germany. Marx did not believe the revolution would come until capitalism had run its course. As wealth was concentrated into fewer and fewer hands, there were not enough people with sufficient money to provide a market. This would lead to major depressions which in turn would lead to a collapse of capitalism. Lenin demonstrated revolutions could be made to occur in less developed countries. The Russians are the victims of their own history. They have had a history of absolute government due largely to the tradition of caesaropapism (the Russian Czar was both head of state and church whereas the European kings shared power with popes and bishops). Politically, the revolution simply communized the absolutist tradition. Lenin and Stalin believed in an elitist, one-party state; not a dictatorship of the proletariat but a dictatorship over the proletariat. This dictatorship has been more concerned with its own power and prestige than in the freedom and welfare of the masses. It has increased consumer production only when it believed it was necessary to do so to keep the populace reasonably happy.

Another reason for the failure of the Marx's theory was the lack of cooperation of the capitalist world. The latter refused to collapse! Thus the communist state could not wither away. It felt impelled to maintain constant war readiness *vis-a-vis* the capitalist camp. B.F. Skinner in **Walden Two** suggests three other reasons for the failure of Soviet utopianisn. First was the decline in the experimental spirit. Once in power, the elite feared any new ideas as subverting their authority. Second was the overpropagandization of Russia. Ideology took precedence over performance. Third was the personality cult. Party and government officials were not free to make objective decisions but had to keep the leader happy.

The Chinese experience in utopia has been both more and less successful than that of the Soviets. Mao Zedung remained a dedicated revolutionary even after he assumed power. He insisted on continuous purification of the revolution and on the purging of party "careerists" or opportunists. The Chinese Communists were exquisitely subtle in their conditioning of the people and so resorted less to coercion than did the Russians. Life in China under Mao would seem to have been similar to that of Puritan New England in which the rank-and-file were intensively zealous. The creation of communes was the most elaborate communitarian experiment that was ever implemented.

For a time, Chinese utopianism was less successful than the Soviet variety. First, the Chinese level of economic development was much lower in 1949 than was that of Russia in 1917. Second, Mao's revolutionary zeal created problems. The Communists had achieved great success in consolidating political power, nationalizing industry, and collectivizing agriculture by the mid-1950s. But Mao was not satisfied with this level of success and so in 1958 instituted the Great Leap Forward, an attempt to radically accelerate the communization and industrialization of China. He succeeded only in throwing the country into economic chaos. Pressured to step aside by more moderate leaders, he immediately began maneuvering to regain power. In the mid-1960s he once again threw China into chaos in what was known as the Cultural Revolution. This was an intensive continuation of the radical-moderate power struggle which had first erupted in 1958. By the early 1970s it appeared that the moderates had regained control. Following the death in 1976 of the leader of the moderates, Zhou Enlai, Mao tried once again to return China to the revolutionary path. This time his own death intervened. After 1977 the moderates under Deng Xiaoping were in control. They introduced what might be called "market socialism" in which the major means of production are still state owned but with many more decisions being made in the marketplace as in capitalistic countries. This is more utopian in that it has increased production but perhaps less utopian in that the gap between the "haves" and "have-nots" has widened.

Sweden is often pictured as a true utopia. According to an article by Michael Malloy, "This is Socialism" in **The National Observer** on March 20, 1976, "Homeowners get loans and tax deductions. Renters get rent subsidies. Parents get children's' allowances. The destitute get subsidized television sets and telephones. College students get stipends, loans, and free tuition. When young couples set up a household, the Bank of Sweden will lend money to furnish it, whether they are married or living in what government publications coyly describe as 'conditions resembling marriage'."

A much different view of Sweden is presented by Roland Huntford in **The New Totalitarians** (1971). At the time he wrote this book, the Social Democratic Party had been in power for almost forty years. Huntford saw Sweden as a corporate state. Decisions were made by a consultative process including the leaders of the party who were also the leaders of the government, the bureaucracy, and representatives of business and labor. According to this view, the parliament was almost as much of a rubber-stamp as is the Supreme Soviet in the Soviet Union. Since Sweden is a code-law country (rights of individuals tend to be subordinated to those of the state), the courts do not have the independence of American courts. Furthermore, Sweden is also a unitary state (all power concentrated in the capitol) and so the educational system is completely dominated by whichever party controls the national government. Radio and television are a government monopoly. Much of the press is subsidized by the government and so tends to follow the party-line. The government encouraged a liberal view towards sex and drugs. In short, Huntford saw Sweden as the "brave new world." He stated, "The price of contentment in Sweden is absolute conformity. Personal desires must be tailored to the desires of the group. Mostly this is forthcoming. Where it is not, society imposes uniformity. Methods are civilized, rational and humane, but still remorseless. Difference in the Swedish world has always been something undesirable, half sin, half disease. In the modern Welfare State, its eradication has become an obsession, because its continued existence is a flaw in the system. " According to this view, the Swede is similar to **The Unknown Citizen** of W.H. Auden. "Was he free? Was he happy? The question is absurd. Had anything been wrong, we should certainly have heard."

Recent events in Sweden partially refute Huntford's argument. Non-socialist governments have been in power. Increasing strikes show something less than complete government control over labor. Polls indicate that many people in Sweden think life is very good.

GLOBALOPIA. In the above section, a number of national utopias were briefly examined. It could be argued that the only true utopia would be a worldwide one. As long as there are national rivalries, there is a danger of war which is certainly not a utopian situation. There have been several attempts, particularly since the end of World War II, to diminish the effect of national boundaries. One of these is the European Common Market. The common market theory is that the economic integration of Europe will make the various countries so interdependent that they will not be able to war with each other anymore than can the fifty American state. Also, the free trade made possible by eliminating of tariffs will encourage more specialization and efficiency. Thus a successful common market will produce both peace and prosperity, two very utopian goals. While the European Common Market has been quite successful, this has not been so true of similar experiments in the Third World (less industrialized countries). The economies of these countries are still primarily agricultural and so there is not a strong basis for trade, particularly since they often produce the same things. Also, while nationalism is decreasing in Europe, it is very much on the increase among the newly-independent countries which want to be independent economically as well as politically.

A second attempt to overcome national barriers has been the United Nations. Politically it has had little success due to Big Power rivalry. In the social and economic field it has experienced some success.

The specialized agencies such as the Food and Agricultural Organization and the World Health Organization have encouraged coöperation. While communists and capitalists may hate each other they also hate being hungry and slapping mosquitoes. But the ideological factor still complicates matters. Communist and capitalist states are often reluctant to contribute much money for fear that the respective agencies may be controlled by persons of the opponent's ideology.

The multinational corporations (MNCs) offer a third possibility. As Richard Barnett and Ronald Mueller say in **Global Reach** (1974), "The men who run the global corporations are the first in history with the organization, technology, money and ideology to make a credible try at managing the world as an integral unit." The authors also note that MNCs bid for the loyalties of several constituencies. They offer (1) better pay to workers, (2) opportunities to local businessmen, (3) assistance to governments to promote economic development, and (4) a higher standard of living to the general public.

The movie **Network** (1976) makes this point very nicely. In the movie, a television commentator is ranting against the increasing financial power of the Arabs in the United States. The network head, who is in the process of obtaining a loan from the Arabs, calls the commentator into his office and makes the following speech: "You have meddled with the primal forces of nature…and I won't have it. Is that clear? You think you have merely stopped a business deal. This is not the case. The Arabs have taken billions of dollars out of this country and now they must put it back. It is ebb and flow, tidal gravity, it is ecological balance. You are an old man who thinks in terms of nations and peoples. There are no nations! There are no peoples! There are no Russians! There are no Arabs! There are no third worlds, there is no West. There is only one holistic system of systems. One vast and immane interwoven, interacting, multivariate, multinational dominion of dollars. Petrodollars, electrodollars, multidollars, reichsmarks, rin, rubles, pounds, and shekels. It is the international system of currency which determines the totality of life on this planet. That is the natural order of things today. That is the atomic and subatomic and galactic structure of things today. You howl about America and democracy. There is no America, there is no democracy. There is only IBM and ITT, AT&T and Dupont, Dow, Union Carbide, and Exxon. Those are the nations of the world today. What do you think the Russians talk about in their councils of state—Karl Marx? They pull out their linear programming charts, statistical decision theories, minimax solutions and compute the price-cost probabilities of their transactions and investments just like we do. We no longer live in a world of nations and ideologies. The world is a business. It has been since man crawled out of the slime and our children will live to see a perfect world in which there is no war or famine, oppression or brutality. One vast and ecumenical holding company for whom all men will work to serve a common profit, in which all men will hold a share of stock, all necessities provided, all anxieties tranquilized, all boredom amused."

According to Barnett and Mueller, the global planners even envisage a "global city." The various MNCs would be headquartered in Paris which would cease to be the capital of France. In this global city there would be no foreigners. Non-French executives of the MNCs living in Paris could vote for the Council of Paris and even be elected to membership. "The global city would, of course, have all the necessary infrastructure (such as) deluxe hotels, conference centers, a telecommunications network,...a University of the World, and a 'financial center'." Three major enemies of the MNCs are organized labor, political leaders, and young people. The first fear the resulting imbalance of power between the business and labor communities. The second see the worldwide corporate attack on "irrational nationalism" as a direct challenge to their own power. The third see all questions (social, racial, cultural, *etcetera*) being subordinated to the consumption ethic and the profit motive. Gulf Oil's support of racist regimes in Africa and ITT's attempts to subvert Chilean politics are but two examples.

CHAPTER SIX

▼

THE DREAM PERVERTED

INTRODUCTION. In the above chapters, a number of fictional and experimental communities were discussed. Whether they were utopias or dystopias depends on the perception of the reader. Utopia, like beauty, is in the eye of the beholder. In this chapter, a brief analysis will be made of several fictional works that are universally considered to be dystopias. One will be discussed which many readers would consider a utopia but which has a dystopian potential. By dystopia is meant a society in which people (1) live under unhappy conditions or (2) have been conditioned to the point where they are no longer creatures of free will.

EVOLUTIONARY DYSTOPIAS. Most utopian and dystopian writers, in creating their fictional societies, position themselves on earth and in the present (give or take a couple hundred years). One category, that of science-fiction writers who sometimes concern themselves with utopian and dystopian questions, often look at the earth from some point in the space and from some point in the far distant future. One such writer was H.G. Wells (**A Modern Utopia** was discussed in Chapter Three). In his book, **The Time Machine** (1895), Wells has a much more pessimistic view of the future. The hero of this book, simply known as the Time Traveler, has invented a machine which enables him to travel forwards and backwards in time. He travels some 800,000 years into the future and discovers a society based on a curious mixture of Marxism and Darwinism.

The first people he meets are the Eloi. They have the appearance of Dresden China dolls, live in a rather run-down communal hall, are vegetarians, and spend their time playing games. In intelligence they are equal to that of five-year old children. Their wants are supplied by a second group of people known as the Morlocks who operate factories underground. The factories had been put there for esthetic purposes. The Morlocks have lived underground so long that they cannot endure sunlight. They surface only at night. They are grotesque in appearance with whitish skin and abnormally large eyes. At first this appears to be an exaggeration of the Countryhouse-Coketown syndrome described by Mumford. The narrator states, "It seemed to me that I had happened upon humanity upon the wane...Under the new conditions of perfect comfort and security, that restless energy, that with us is strength, would become weakness. Even in our time certain tendencies and desires, once necessary to survival, are a constant source of failure. Physical courage and the love of battle, for instance, are no great help—may even be hindrances—to a civilized man. And in a state of physical balance and security, power, intellectual as well as physical, would be out of place. For countless years I judged there had been no danger of war or solitary violence, no danger from wild beasts, no wasting diseases to require strength of constitution, no need of toil. For such a life, what we should call the weak are as well equipped as the strong, are indeed no longer weak. Better equipped indeed they are, for the strong would be fretted by an energy for which there was no outlet. No doubt the exquisite beauty of the buildings I saw was the outcome of the last surgings of the now purposeless energy of mankind before it settled down into perfect harmony with the conditions under which it lived, the flourish of that triumph which began the last great peace. This has ever been the fate of energy in security; it takes to art and to eroticism, and then come languor and decay."

As the plot develops, the Morlocks turn out to be the dominant group. They are cannibals and so provide for the Eloi as farmers do for their cattle. A long departure from Plato when society is ruled not by philosopher-kings but by vicious animal-like creatures. This is not exactly what Marx had in mind by the dictatorship of the proletariat.

Another science-fiction writer with this long-term view of the future was Olaf Stapledon. In the **Last and First Men** (1930), he views the world from a point over a billion years in the future. Man has gone through numerous evolutions. At one point, the Fifth Men were capable of telepathic communications with one another. "The result was that, though conflict of wills was still possible, it was far more easily resolved by mutual understanding than had been the case in earlier species. Thus there were no lasting and no radical conflicts, either of thought or desire. It was universally recognized that every discrepancy of opinion and of aim could be abolished by telepathic discussion." This would indeed be utopia. For the most part, however, the book gives a rather dystopian and pessimistic view of the future. The Fifth Men discover that the moon's orbit is diminishing and that the moon will eventually crash into the earth. They build space ships and escape to Venus. (This theme of interplanetary travel to escape a catastrophe on earth appears again in Walter Miller's **Canticle for Leibowitz** .) Three cycles later, the Eighth Men discover that the sun will flare up making life on the planets impossible and so they go to Neptune. At the end of the book, the Seventeenth Men are calmly awaiting extinction having discovered that life even on Neptune will become extinct. The narrator concludes, "Throughout all his existence man has been striving to hear the music of the spheres, and has seemed to himself once and again to catch some phrase of it, or even a hint of the whole form of it. Yet he can never be sure that he has truly heard it, nor even that there is any such perfect music at all to be heard. Inevitably so, for if it exists, it is not for him in his littleness. But one thing is certain. Man himself, at the very least, is music, a brave theme that makes music also of its vast accompaniment, its matrix of storms and stars. Man himself in his degree is eternally a beauty in the eternal form of things. It is very good to have been man. And so we may go forward together with laughter in our hearts, and peace, thankful for the past and for our own courage. For we shall make after all a fair conclusion to this brief music that is man." Despair perhaps, but noble despair.

The notion of the evolution of man into a utopian superörganism is also found in The **Phenomenon of Man** (1959) by Pierre Teilhard de Chardin. "The noösphere tends to constitute a single closed system in which each element sees, feels, desires, and suffers for itself the same things as all the others at the same time. We are faced with a harmonized collectivity of consciousness equivalent to a sort of super-consciousness. The idea is that of the earth not only becoming covered by myriads of grains of thought, but becoming enclosed in a single thinking envelope so as to form, functionally, no more than a single vast grain of thought on the sidereal scale, the plurality of individual reflections grouping themselves together and reinforcing one another in the act of a single unanimous reflection." The lack of privacy and individuality entailed is common in many dystopias.

BEHAVIORALISTIC DYSTOPIAS. In Chapter One, one of the suggested characteristics of the utopias was the belief that man is malleable. Most utopists believe simultaneously that man can shape his environment but that he is also shaped by it. They see a two-step process: (1) the elite creates a favorable environment for utopia, and (2) the rank-and-file members of the community then respond to this new environment. This approach is particularly evident in **Walden Two** and the **Brave New World**. Both can be seen as utopias in that people are happy and yet they can also be seen as dystopias for, in both, man is no longer a creature of free will.

This is the theme of **Walden Two** (1948) by B.F. Skinner. It is his contention that the sure way to create utopia is through behavioral engineering. The Walden Two founder, Frazier, says "if it's in our power to create any of the situations which a person likes or to remove any situation he doesn't like, we can control his behavior....I deny that freedom exists at all. I must deny it—or my program would be absurd. You can't have a science about a subject matter which hops capriciously about. Perhaps we can never prove that man isn't free; it's an assumption. But the increasing success of a science of behavior makes it more and more plausible....Our members are practically always doing what they want to do—what they 'choose' to do—but we see to it that they want to do precisely the things which are best for themselves and the community. Their behavior is determined, yet they're free. "One of the methods in conditioning children is to give them lollipops with powdered sugar on them so a single touch of the tongue can be detected. They are told they may eat them later in the day if they have not already been licked. Another method is to require children, after a long walk, to stand for five minutes before a steaming bowl of hot soup.

The hierarchy of Walden Two consists of Planners and Managers. The original Planners were appointed by the founder and created a class of Managers who were hired and promoted on the basis of merit. When a vacancy occurs on the Board of Planners, the Planners choose the replacement from two candidates nominated by the Managers. As in many utopias, there is a self-perpetuating elite. As Frazier states, "It (democracy) isn't, and can't be, the best form of government, because it's based on a scientifically invalid conception of man. It fails to take account of the fact that in the long run man is determined by the state. A *laissez-faire* philosophy which trusts to the inherent goodness and wisdom of the common man is incompatible with the observed fact that men are made good or bad and wise or foolish by the environment in which they grow." While Frazier denies the validity of democracy, he does not feel Walden Two is completely antidemocratic. "The people have all the voice they have any need for. They can accept or protest—and much more effectively than in a democracy, let me add. And we all share equally in the common wealth, which is the intention but not the achievement of the democratic program. Anyone born into Walden

Two has a right to any place among us for which he can demonstrate the necessary talent or ability."

From the economic standpoint, people are assigned various tasks for which they receive labor credits. These credits can then be used to pay for whatever goods and services are used. Food and clothing are made in the most practical way possible. "The commercial baker tries to produce a satisfactory loaf with the fewest and cheapest materials. Here the goal is in the other direction. Our cooks have to prepare the food we produce so that it will be eaten. They want to get as much into a loaf of bread as possible." Another character says, "We simply choose the kind of clothes which suffer the slowest change—suits, sweaters and shirts, or blouses and skirts, and so on." The educational system was progressive. "We teach only the techniques of learning and thinking. As for geography, literature, the sciences—we give our children opportunity and guidance, and they learn them for themselves." History, even the history of Walden Two, is very much discouraged. "The founding of Walden Two is never recalled publicly by anyone who took part in it. No distinction of seniority is recognized." When asked if community life did not discourage personal ambitions, Frazier replies, "What does 'making a name for himself mean?' Do you mean making a fortune? We have no need for fortunes, and until you can show me how a fortune can be made without making a few paupers in the bargain, it's the goal we're glad to do without. Fame is also at the expense of others. When one man gets a place in the sun, others are put in a denser shade. From the point of view of the whole group there's no gain whatsoever, and perhaps a loss."

Like the original Walden, Walden Two was an experiment in living, thus its name. It is as much of a utopia as any of the others discussed. Yet one is left with the uneasy feeling that a dystopia is just around the corner. The author seems confident that the Planners will not be corrupted by power and yet Lord Acton's maxim—Power tends to corrupt and absolute power tends to corrupt absolutely—cannot be easily dismissed. Is there a clear boundary between **Walden Two** and the **Brave New World** (1932) of Aldous Huxley?

In the latter work, the entire world has come under the control of a dictatorship some six hundred years in the future. There are ten World Controllers, one of which—Mustafa Mond—is a major character in the book. The slogan is Community—Identity—Stability. The emphasis is on stability with a place for everybody (identity) and everybody in his place (community). Genetic engineering has been taken to the ultimate. Through the Bokanovsky Process, eggs are taken from the human female and can be made to produce as many as ninety-six children. Here Huxley seems to anticipate the "cloning" of lower forms of animal life now being done in some laboratories. Children are not born but "decanted." By varying the oxygen supply to the fetus, a caste system is created ranging from the Alphas to the Epsilons. "The optimum population," says Mustafa Mond, "is modeled on the iceberg: eight-ninths below the water line, one-ninth above." The purpose of all of this prenatal conditioning is "making people like their inescapable social destiny."

People are also kept happy by being given an abundance of material goods. "Ending is better than mending. The more stitches, the less riches." Henry Ford, because he developed the assembly line method which made possible the technological abundance of the modern world, has become the god of the society. He is also worshipped because he said, "History is bunk." As noted in Chapter One, utopias are generally disinterested in history since they look more to the future. Instead of crosses, people wear T's around their necks, symbolizing the Model T.

Gratification of every sensual desire is encouraged. There are, for example, "feelies" which involve all of the senses, not simply sound and vision as do our movies. Sex is completely permissive. Women who have not been sterilized (those who have are called Freemartins) engage in something called Malthusian Drill so there won't be any unexpected pregnancies. To be born directly from the mother instead of from the test-tube is considered degrading. Periodically people engage in Solidarity Services, a perversion of the Christian sacrament of holy communion. Soma, a mild drug, takes the place of the bread and wine. The participants sing a Solidarity Hymn of which the first and last stanzas are given below:

> Ford, we are twelve; oh, make us one,
> like drops within the Social River;
> Oh, make us now together run
> as swiftly as thy shining Flivver.

> Orgy-porgy, Ford and fun,
> kiss the girls and make them One.
> Boys at one with girls at peace;
> orgy-porgy gives release.

In the **Brave New World** there are savages who live on reservations. One of these is a major character in the book. Known simply as the Savage, he has some interesting discussions with Mustafa Mond. He is very fond of Shakespeare and asks why the people might not be permitted to see Othello. (He came across the book accidentally since most such books had been destroyed or were locked up.) Mustafa Mond replies, "Because our world is not the same as Othello's world. You can't make flivvers without steel—and you can't make tragedies without social instability. The world's stable now. People are happy; they get what they want, and they never want what they can't get. They're well off; they're blissfully ignorant of passion and old age; they're plagued with no mothers or fathers; they've got no wives, or children, or lovers to feel strongly about; they're so conditioned that they practically can't help behaving as they ought to behave. And if anything should go wrong, there's soma."

Although not denying the existence of God, Mustafa Mond believes that He manifests Himself as an absence, as though He weren't there at all. "Call it the fault of civilization. God isn't compatible with machinery and scientific medicine and universal happiness." Furthermore, a God generally demands sacrifice. "But industrial civilization is only possible when there's no self-denial. Self-indulgence up to the very limits imposed by hygiene and economics. Otherwise the wheels stop turning." The Savage asks if it isn't natural to believe in God when we're alone at night, thinking about death. "But people never are alone now," says Mustafa Mond. "We make them hate solitude, and we arrange their lives so that it's almost impossible for them ever to have it." Not only is there no solitude but not even family life. "Our Ford, or our Freud, as, for some inscrutable reason, he chooses to call himself whenever he spoke of psychological matters—Our Freud had been the first to reveal the appalling dangers of family life. The world was full of fathers: was therefore full of misery; full of mothers: therefore full of every kind of perversion from sadism to chastity; full of brothers, sisters, uncles, aunts: full of madness and suicide."

Still another passage is reminiscent of Skinner. "Civilization has absolutely no need of nobility or heroism. These things are symptoms of political inefficiency. In a properly organized society like ours, nobody has any opportunities for being noble or heroic." The Savage concludes by "claiming the right to be unhappy...the right to grow old and ugly and impotent; the right to have syphilis and cancer; the right to have too little to eat; the right to be lousy; the right to live in constant apprehension of what may happen tomorrow; the right to catch typhoid; the right to be tortured by unspeakable pains of every kind."

In the final chapter, the Savage is exiled to an island. At first he is left alone but then tourists come to view him and ridicule him. He ultimately commits suicide by hanging himself. "Slowly, very slowly, like two unhurried compass needles, the feet turned toward the right; north, northeast, east, southeast, south, southwest; then paused, and after a few seconds turned as unhurriedly back towards the left. Southwest, south, southeast, east...."

In 1958, Huxley wrote **Brave New World Revisited**. In this he sees many of his fears being at least partially realized. He is concerned about overpopulation which leads to over-centralization and over-propagandization. He is concerned about the modern techniques of conditioning people such as "brainwashing," chemical persuasion, and subconscious persuasion. He suggests education as one means to prevent the brave new world from coming. "Individuals must be suggestible enough to be willing and able to make their society work but not so suggestible as to fall helpless under the spell of professional mind-manipulators."

The mechanical robots of Karel Capek's play, **R.U.R.** or **Rossum's Universal Robots,** first presented in 1921, are in many ways more admirable creatures than the human robots of the **Brave New World.** In this play, man has been so dehumanized that it is virtually impossible to distinguish humans from robots. To make them less cold, the "nervous irritability" of the robots is increased. This causes them to revolt. One cannot imagine a revolt among the Epsilons.

TOTALITARIAN DYSTOPIAS. We turn now to outright dystopias. Whatever their economic arrangements, whether capitalistic or socialistic, they are politically fascist. The individual is totally subordinated to the state. This point is made in **Crucible Island** (1919) by Conde B. Pallen. Children are taught the following catechism:

> 1. By whom were you begotten? By the sovereign State.
> 2. Why were you begotten? That I might know, love and serve the Sovereign State.
> 3. What is the Sovereign State? The Sovereign State is Humanity in composite and perfect being.
> 4. Why is the State supreme? The State is supreme because it is my Creator and Conserver, in which I am and move and have my being and without which I am nothing.

5. What is the individual? The individual is only a part of the whole, and made for the whole, and finds his complete and perfect expressionin the Sovereign State. Individuals are made for cooperation only like feet, hands, eyelids, like the rows of upper and lower teeth.

The two major dystopias discussed here are **We** or *Nous Autres* (1924) by Eugene Zamiatin and **Nineteen Eighty-Four** (1949) by George Orwell. Zamiatin was a Russian revolutionary who was appalled by the police-state being created by Lenin. Both works depict completely bureaucratized societies. The plot line of the latter was very similar to that of the former.

In **We**, the time is a thousand years in the future. The entire world is organized into a single political system known as the United State. The ruler is known as the Well-Doer. Once a year he is "re-elected" on Unanimity Day. He occasionally appears in public to execute political criminals. Execution is by an electrolytic process whereby the human body is dissolved into a pool of water. The Well-Doer is assisted by a secret police known as the Bureau of Guardians. There are special membranes handsomely decorated and placed over all avenues, registering all street conversations for the Bureau of Guardians.

Individuality has become totally destroyed. "We" is from God, "I" is from the devil. Citizens are known simply by numbers. Everyone lives in glass houses and lives his daily life according to rigid schedules known as the Tables. "We have nothing to conceal from one another; besides, this mode of living makes the difficult and exalted task of the Guardians much easier. Without it many bad things might happen. It is possible that the strange opaque dwellings of the ancients were responsible for their pitiful cellish psychology....I have had opportunity to read and hear many improbable things about those times when human beings still lived in the state of freedom; that is, in an unorganized primitive state. One thing has always seemed to me most improbable: how could a government, even a primitive government, permit people to live without anything like our Tables: without compulsory walks, without precise regulation of the time to eat, for instance? They would get up and go to bed whenever they liked. Some historians even say that in those days the streets were lighted all night, and all night people went about the streets."

Sex is also minutely regulated. "You are carefully examined in the laboratory of the Sexual Department where they find the content of the sexual hormones in your blood, and they accordingly make out for you a table of sexual days. Then you file an application to enjoy the services of Number so and so, or Numbers so and so. You get for that purpose a check slip. That is all." Privacy is permitted during the "sex hours" when the shades may be drawn. The purpose of all this, of course, is to destroy love.

People live in large cities screened off from rural areas by Green Walls (possibly glass domes to control the weather). "It is clear that the history of mankind, as far as our knowledge goes, is a history of the transition from nomadic forms to more sedentary ones. Does it not follow that the most sedentary form of life (ours) is at the same time the most perfect one? There was a time when people rushed from one end of the earth to another, but this was the prehistoric time when such things as nations, wars, commerce, different discoveries of different Americas still existed. Who has need of these things now?" Nature has been almost completely annihilated. People eat synthetic foods and wear clothing made of synthetic fibers (not as common in 1924 as now).

The hero is D-503, an engineer working on a spaceship to be used to colonize other planets. He has been utterly conditioned to accept the regimentation of life. Who would want to be liberated? "It is remarkable how persistent human criminal instincts are! I use deliberately the word 'criminal,' for freedom and crime are as closely related as—well, as the movement of an aero(plane) and its speed: if the speed of an aero equals zero, the aero is motionless; if human liberty is equal to zero, man does not commit any crime. That is clear. The way to rid man of criminality is to rid him of freedom." His girl-friend, I-330, is a revolutionary. There are other revolutionaries living in the wilderness areas between the cities, similar to the reservations of the Brave new World. These revolutionaries are trying to capture the spaceship to escape to another planet. D-503 thinks I-330 is absurd "because a revolution is impossible!...Because our...revolution was the last one." I-330 responds that just as there cannot be such a thing as a last number, so there cannot be a last revolution. "...their number is infinite...The 'last one' is a child's story. Children are afraid of the infinite, and it is necessary that children should not be frightened, so that they may sleep through the night."

In the conclusion, D-503, along with most other citizens, has agreed to submit to a lobotomy-type operation which destroys the "center for fancy." This operation almost literally reduces people to human robots. He calmly watches as I-330, who has been captured by the authorities, is placed in a vacuum chamber from which all air is removed.

The above work has a science-fiction quality about it which makes it a little incredible and therefore not quite so frightening as is *1984*. Orwell's book is a description of life in Stalinist Russia or Nazi Germany. He pictures a world that has existed and still exists in parts of the world today. The world is comprised of three dictatorships. Oceana represents the absorption of Latin America, the United States, Australasia, and the southern part of Africa by Britain. Eurasia emerged with the absorption of Europe by Russia. Eastasia consists mainly of China and Japan. The ideologies of the three dictatorships are respectively Ingsoc (English Socialism), Neo-Bolshevism, and Death-Worship or the Obliteration of Self.

Within Oceana, there is a rigid hierarchy headed by Big Brother. (It is not clear whether Big Brother is an actual person or simply a symbol for a collective dictatorship.) Below him is the Inner Party and the Outer Party, similar to the division in the Soviet Union between the elite and the general membership. At the bottom are the "proles." The government consists of four ministries: (1) the Ministry of Peace (Minipeace) responsible for the conduct of war; (2) the Ministry of Plenty (Miniplenty) administering the rationing system; (3) the Ministry of Truth (Minitruth) disseminating propaganda; and (4) the Ministry of Love (Minilove) administering the secret police system.

Newspeak and Doublethink are two major concepts. "The purpose of Newspeak was not only to provide a medium of expression for...the devotees of Ingsoc, but to make all other modes of thought impossible."…Doublethink means the power of holding two contradictory beliefs in one's mind simultaneously, and accepting both of them. The Party intellectual knows in which direction his memories must be altered; he therefore knows that he is playing tricks with reality; but by the exercise of doublethink he also satisfies himself that reality is not violated. The process has to be conscious, or it would not be carried out with sufficient precision, but it also has to be unconscious, or it would bring with it a feeling of falsity and hence of guilt." An example might be the position Soviet party types were in when Khrushchev denounced the "crimes" of Stalin, the man who previously had been considered infallible.

Three slogans represent the ideology of Oceana. The first of these is, **WAR IS PEACE.** The three dictatorships are constantly at war with each other. This war takes place in a relatively neutral zone spreading from northern Africa through the Middle East to India and Southeastern Asia. There is some contradiction in Emanuel Goldstein, the leader of the underground opposition. He says that "The two aims of the party are to conquer the whole surface of the earth and to extinguish once and for all the possibility of independent thought" but implies that the real purpose of the war is to enable each of the three governments to justify their dictatorships. "The essential act of war is destruction…of the products of human labor,…materials which might otherwise be used to make the masses too comfortable, and hence, in the long run, too intelligent." War "eats up the surplus of consumable goods, and it helps to preserve the special mental atmosphere that a hierarchical society needs." (Paradoxically, the **Brave New World** is a dictatorship that rests on abundance.) "The war is waged by each ruling group against its own subjects, and the object of the war is…to keep the structure of society intact. The very word 'war,' therefore, has become misleading. It would probably be more accurate to say that by becoming continuous war has ceased to exist....This is the inner meaning of the Party slogan: War is Peace."

The second slogan is, **IGNORANCE IS STRENGTH**. Oceana is based on the premise that there cannot be strong government without an infallible leader which in turn requires an ignorant people. "Oceanic society rests ultimately on the belief that Big Brother is omnipotent and that the Party is infallible. But since in reality Big Brother is not omnipotent and the party is not infallible, there is a need for an unwearying, moment-to-moment flexibility in the treatment of the facts....This demands a continuous alteration of the past." This is necessary so that the Party member will have no basis of comparison with earlier times and also because no change in doctrine or in political alignment can ever be admitted. "If, for example, Eurasia or Eastasia is the enemy today, than that country must always have been the enemy." History is constantly being rewritten. (This has happened many times in the Soviet Union.) "The mutability of the past is the central tenet of Ingsoc. Past events, it is argued, have no objective existence, but survive only in written records and in human memories. The past is whatever the records and the memories agree upon. Since the Party is in full control of all records, and in equally full control of the minds of its members, it follows that the past is whatever the Party chooses to make it."

The third slogan is, **FREEDOM IS SLAVERY**. "Alone—free—the human being is always defeated. It must be so, because every human being is doomed to die, which is the greatest of all failures. But if he make complete, utter submission, if he can escape from his identity, if he can merge himself in the Party so that he is the Party, then he is all-powerful and immortal." Power is asserted by making the people suffer. "Children will be taken from their mothers at birth, as one takes eggs from a hen. The sex instinct will be eradicated. Procreation will be an annual formality like the renewal of a ration card. We shall abolish the orgasm. Our neurologists are at work on it now. There will be no loyalty, except loyalty toward the Party. There will be no love, except the love of Big Brother, no laughter, except the laugh of triumph over a defeated enemy. There will be no art, no literature, no science. When we are omnipotent we shall have no more need of science. There will be no distinction between beauty and ugliness. There will be no curiosity, no employment of the process of life. All competing pleasures will be destroyed. But always...there will be the intoxication of power, constantly increasing and constantly growing subtler, the sensation of trampling on an enemy who is helpless. If you want a picture of the future, imagine a boot stamping on a human face—forever."

The plot line is similar to that of **We**. In place of D-503 and I-330 are Winston Smith and Julia. Like the former they engage in revolutionary activity and are caught. Winston, too, is brainwashed and calmly watches Julia being tortured. "He gazed up at the enormous face (Big Brother). Forty years it had taken him to learn what kind of smile was hidden beneath the dark mustache. O cruel, needless misunderstanding! O stubborn, self-willed exile from the loving breast! Two gin-scented tears trickled down the sides of his nose. But it was all right, everything was all right, the struggle was finished. He had won the victory over himself. He loved Big Brother."

How close are we to 1984? In some ways, much closer than is comfortable to admit. During the Vietnamese War and Watergate, the government engaged in a kind of Doublethink. President Nixon, for example, was faced with the dilemma of having to know what was going on in order to be in command of events and having not to know so that he could be more credible when he denied things. In national security matters, governments do believe that "ignorance is strength." David Wiseman in **The Politics of Lying** (1973) points out numerous examples of government deception, not always necessitated by national security requirements. Likewise "war is peace" when both we and the Russians spent hundreds of billions of dollars per year for a war each hoped would never happen. Finally, in the welfare state, "freedom is slavery" for while we are freer from economic concerns we are steadily losing control over our personal lives. As for Newspeak, "wasting" people does not sound as bad as killing them, terminating a pregnancy does not sound as bad as killing a fetus.

The above dystopias are statist but not racist or sexist. The dystopia in **Swastika Night** (1937) by Murray Constantine is all three as indicated in the following poem:

> As a woman is above a worm,
> So is a man above a woman.
> As a man is above a woman,
> So is a Nazi above any foreign Hitlerian.
> As a Nazi is above a foreign Hitlerian,
> So is a Knight above a Nazi.
> As a Knight is above a Nazi,

So is *Der Fuehrer* (whom may Hitler bless)
Above all Knights.

The author was warning as to what might have happened if Hitler had not been defeated. The slogan of Hitler's dystopia was, ***Ein Volk, Ein Reich, Ein Führer.*** The world was to be dominated by the German Superstate which was controlled by the Aryan Superrace (the creators of culture) which in turn was dominated by the Nazi Supermen who were driven by a Nietzschean will to power.

CHAPTER SEVEN

▼

THE DREAM REVISITED

IS THE DREAM POSSIBLE? In attempting to answer this question, one tends to get bogged down in semantics. Is utopia a "no-place"? If so, the answer is no for a "no-place" cannot be "someplace." Is utopia a perfect place? If so, again, the dream is not possible for as Thomas Molnar states in **Utopia: The Perennial Heresy** (1967), "The truth is that society is always unfinished, always in motion and its key problems can never be solved by social engineering." If we define utopia as a perfect place, presumably that means the absence of all problems. But would not that itself be a problem?

If we merely define utopia as a good place, "How good is good?" But let us not quibble over semantics but simply assume that utopia is a good place if somewhat short of perfection. Do we have the material resources to create utopia? In an age when we are exhausting fossil fuels, the answer to that question seems more and more doubtful. Utopia may be possible for a few chosen countries but can it be possible on a worldwide basis. And if not, is it utopia? The answer might be more affirmative should we enforce rigorous conservation policies and simultaneously reduce our expectations.

Do we have the intelligence to create utopia? We do to create bigger and better bombs and to put men into space but we have not done so well with social and economic questions. After World War II we thought we no longer had to fear a worldwide depression and yet now the specter hangs over our heads.

Even more crucial, do we have the will to create utopia? Here too the answer is in doubt. We probably do have the resources and intelligence to solve our energy crisis but so far have not found the will to mobilize ourselves to get on with the task. Then too, there is what might be called the "law of reverse effect." How often do things work out the way we planned? Planning agencies often rigidify into stagnant bureaucracies. Democratic politics degenerates into machine politics. Attempts to correct discrimination often lead to reverse discrimination.

One thing does seem certain, no matter how we define utopia it is not possible without a spirit of altruism. Socialist utopias with the formula, "From each according to his ability, to each according to his need," require a great deal of altruism. Even capitalism without some spirit of altruism degenerates into a dog-eat-dog life style. It would seem fair to say that some kind of religious basis is necessary to promote the required degree of altruism.

IS THE DREAM DESIRABLE? The answer to this question is surely "yes" when we think of the alternatives. The Savage in the **Brave New World** wanted the right to be sick but once sick he would want the right to be well. Surely we can find challenges other than obtaining adequate food, shelter, clothing, and medical care.

Yet there are strong arguments to the contrary. As Don Juan says in **Man and Superman** by G.B. Shaw, "Hell is the home of the unreal and of the seekers of happiness. It is the only refuge from heaven, which is, as I tell you, the home of the masters of reality, and from earth, which is the home of the slaves of reality.... Hell, in short, is a place where you have nothing to do but amuse yourself."

Molnar (cited earlier) believes that from a theological viewpoint, utopia is not desirable. "At utopia's roots there is a defiance of God, pride unlimited, a yearning for enormous power and the assumption of divine attributes with a view to manipulating and shaping mankind's fate. The utopian is not content with pressing men into a mold of his own manufacture; he is not a mere despot, dictator or totalitarian leader holding all temporal and spiritual power. His real vice is, first, the desire to dismantle human individuality through the dissolution of individual conscience and consciousness, and then to replace these with the collectivity and coalesced consciousness. In a raving moment Caligula wished that mankind had only one head so that he might chop it off with one blow. So too, the utopian: he wants to deal with only one entity so as to simplify his own task of transforming indomitable human nature into a slave. What the utopian conceives of as the future, fabulous as it may seem, is, in reality, a nightmare. It could not be otherwise because the utopian, in his speculation, ignores human nature, the rhythm of change, the fact that change involves not only gain but loss as well, the reality of time and the essential freedom of the soul. It is noteworthy that while, at least in the world-view of our western religions, Almighty God created man with a free will, the utopian makes the human condition so rigid that freedom is excluded from utopia. He replaces the concept of divine providence with unchangeable determinism." For Molnar, the utopian prototype is not Plato's Philosopher-King, but rather Dostoyevsky's Grand Inquisitor as depicted in **The Brothers Karamazov.**

One may further raise the question as to whether the attainment of heaven on earth is a barrier to the attainment of the ultimate heaven. Marx said that religion was the opiate of the masses but in utopia the opiates of ease and comfort become the religion of the masses. In utopia, God is replaced by society and the state but false gods, unlike the true one, cannot offer grace.

REDEFINITION OF UTOPIA. In attempting a redefinition of utopia, perhaps we, too, must engage in some Doublethink. Utopia is both possible and impossible, desirable and undesirable, orthodoxy and heresy. In the final analysis, utopia is never the destination but the journey. As God says in the prologue to Goethe's **Faust,** "The one who continuously keeps striving is the one who can be saved." In that spirit, the poem **Ode** by Arthur O'Shaughnessy is a fitting tribute to the utopists:

We are the music-makers, and we are the dreamers of dreams,
Wandering by lone sea-breakers, and sitting by desolate streams

World-losers and world-forsakers, on whom the pale moon gleams:
Yet we are the movers and shakers of the world forever, it seems.

With wonderful deathless ditties we build up the world's great cities,
And out of a fabulous story we fashion an empire's glory:
One man with a dream, at pleasure, shall go forth and conquer
    a crown;
And three with a new song's measure can trample an empire down.

We, in the ages lying in the buried past of the earth,
Built Nineveh with our sighing, and Babel itself with our mirth;
And o'erthrew them with prophesying to the old of the new
    world's worth,
For each age is a dream that is dying, or one that is coming to birth.

About the Author

A Korean War veteran, the author also served as an American diplomatic officer in Indonesia, Hong Kong, and briefly with the House Appropriations Committee of the U.S. Congress. For over thirty years he taught political theory and comparative government in the Minnesota State University System at St. Cloud State University.

BIBLIOGRAPHY

SELECTED UTOPIAN AND DYSTOPIAN WORKS: PRIMARY

Andreae, Johann, **Christianopolis** (1620).

Aristophanes, **Ecclesiazusae** (c. 393 BC).

Augustine, **The City of God** (426).

Bacon, Francis, **New Atlantis** (1627).

Bellamy, Edward, **Looking Backward** (1888).

Bulwer-Lytton, Edward, **The Coming Race** (1871).

Burgess, Anthony, **A Clockwork Orange** (1962).

Butler, Samuel, **Erewhon** (1872).

Cabet, Etienne, **Voyage to Icaria** (1840).

Campanella, Tommaso, **The City of the Sun** (1623).

Churchward, James, **The Lost Continent of Mu** (1931).

Constantine, Murray, **Swastika Night** (1937).

Donnelly, Ignatius, **Caesar's Column** (1890).

Golding, William, **Lord of the Flies** (1954).

Harrington, James, **The Commonwealth of Oceana** (1656).

Hertzka, Theodor, **Freeland** (1891).

House, Edward, **Philip Dru: Administrator** (1912).

Hunt, Haroldson, **Alpaca** (1960).

Huxley, Aldous, **Brave New World** (1932).
     Island (1962).
London, Jack, **The Iron Heel** (1907).
More, Thomas, **Utopia** (1516).
Morris, William, **News from Nowhere** (1890).
Orwell, George, **Nineteen Eighty-Four** (1949).
Owen, Robert, **A New View of Society** (1812).
Pallen, Conde, **Crucible Island** (1919).
Peter, Lawrence, **The Peter Plan** (1976).
Plato, **The Republic** (c. 387 BC).
Rand, Ayn, **Atlas Shrugged** (1957).
Skinner, Burrhus Frederic, **Walden Two** (1948).
Stapledon, Olaf, **Last and First Men** (1930).
Swift, Jonathan, **Gulliver's Travels** (1726).
Vonnegut, Kurt, **Player Piano** (1952).
Wells, Herbert George, **A Modern Utopia** (1905).
     The Time Machine (1895).
     Men Like Gods (1923).
Wright, Austin, **Islandia** (1942).
Zamiatin, Eugene, **We** or *Nous Autres* (1924).

SECONDARY WORKS

Armytage, Walter, **Heavens Below** (1960).
    Yesterday's Tomorrows (1968).
Berneri, Maria, **A Journey Through Utopia** (1950).
Bestor, Arthur, **Backwoods Utopias** (1950).
Bierce, Ambrose, **The Devil's Dictionary** (1911).
Calverton, Vernon, **Where Angels Dared to Tread** (1941).
Hertzler, Joyce, **The History of Utopian Thought** (1923).
Holloway, Mark, **Heavens on Earth** (1951).
Molnar, Thomas, **Utopia: The Perennial Heresy** (1967).
Morgan, Arthur, **Nowhere was Somewhere** (1946).
Mumford, Lewis, **The Story of Utopias** (1922).
Nordhoff, Charles, **Communistic Societies of the United States** (1875).
Noyes, John, **History of American Socialisms** (1870).
Spiro, Melford, **Kibbutz: Venture in Utopia** (1956).
Teilhard de Chardin, Pierre, **Phenomenon of Man** (1959).
Walsh, Chad, **From Utopia to Nightmare** (1962).
Webber, Everett, **Escape to Utopia** (1959).

9 780595 183913